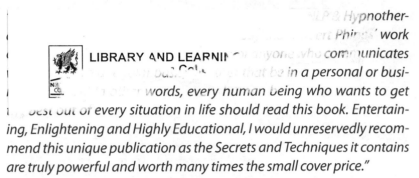
... NLP & Hypnother-
... Phipps' work
... anyone who communicates
... that be in a personal or busi-
... words, every human being who wants to get
... best out of every situation in life should read this book. Entertaining, Enlightening and Highly Educational, I would unreservedly recommend this unique publication as the Secrets and Techniques it contains are truly powerful and worth many times the small cover price."

Dr. Jonathan Royle, www.magicalguru.com

"Recognising what you – and others – are doing with body language turns 'instinct' into powerful knowledge. In this book Robert Phipps can help us all, at work and play, use body language to our advantage. Even learning one thing, such as looking above the bridge of someone's nose, could make a difference… read and see how."

Gill Cox, Agony aunt

"Robert's understanding of his subject is deep and thorough – he knows what he's writing about. Plus, he can communicate that knowledge, so that every reader can put it into practice and have it make an immediate difference to everyday life. Clear, helpful, packed full of facts, insights and interactive exercises, this is the book you need if you want to master body language."

**Susan Quilliam, Psychologist and Agony Aunt
for numerous media including AOL**

"This book is crammed with treasures which throw light on a much-misunderstood topic. The easy, conversational style makes it a pleasure to read, and the focus on practical application provides numerous examples which are sure to resonate with anyone who works intensively with people. I shall undoubtedly be dipping in again and again for guidance on how best to navigate the plethora of interpersonal obstacles which crop up on a daily basis. ... This is long overdue."

... nan, Investec Bank

BODY LANGUAGE

It's What You Don't Say That Matters

Robert Phipps

CAPSTONE

This edition first published 2012

© 2012 Robert Phipps

Registered office

John Wiley & Sons Ltd, The Atrium, Southern Gate, Chichester, West Sussex, PO19 8SQ, United Kingdom

For details of our global editorial offices, for customer services and for information about how to apply for permission to reuse the copyright material in this book please see our website at www.wiley.com.

Wiley publishes in a variety of print and electronic formats and by print-on-demand. Some material included with standard print versions of this book may not be included in e-books or in print-on-demand. If this book refers to media such as a CD or DVD that is not included in the version you purchased, you may download this material at http://booksupport.wiley.com. For more information about Wiley products, visit www.wiley.com.

Library of Congress Cataloging-in-Publication Data (to follow)

ISBN 9780857081742 (paperback)   ISBN 9780857082084 (ebk)

ISBN 9780857082091 (ebk)   ISBN 9780857082909 (ebk)

A catalogue record for this book is available from the British Library.

Set in 11/15 pt Myriad Pro by Sparks, UK – www.sparkspublishing.com

Printed in Great Britain by TJ International Ltd, Padstow, Cornwall, UK

CONTENTS

PART ONE

THE BODY OF EVIDENCE

ARE YOU SITTING COMFORTABLY?

Are you aware of the expression on your face right now? Are you aware of how you're sitting or standing, or who and what is around you?

Probably not – until I asked the question and your brain went to do a little check, or you had a look round.

Most people are oblivious, most of the time, to what their body is doing.

If you are one of these people, you'll be unaware just how much your body tells others about you. About your moods, emotions and attitudes.

These body movements, signals and gestures are forms of non-verbal communication, or what we commonly refer to as 'body language'.

In business, being aware of and understanding this subject can dramatically change people's perceptions of you – and consequently the results you achieve.

This book takes you through everyday business situations, pointing out what to observe, what to do with what you see, and how to turn it to your advantage.

I start right at the beginning with what body language is, and then take you through greetings, meetings, presenting, selling, negotiating, managing, leading and all the other key areas you need to understand in your business to make the best decisions and be successful.

Over the course of this book, I'll cover all of the situations and common behaviours, just as you would encounter them in your business and your personal life. By the end, you'll be an expert at interpreting what body language means in different situations, and you'll have a range of techniques and approaches to deal with people depending on the signals you see them exhibiting.

BODY LANGUAGE AND THE UNCONSCIOUS

Body language is ubiquitous and affects us all – through our interactions with family, friends, colleagues, shop and restaurant staff, and government officials like police and traffic wardens. They all send us silent messages that tell us things about them, their job and how they feel.

I'm sure you can remember characteristics about certain people you've come into contact with throughout your life: a particular teacher who had a funny walk when you were knee high to a grasshopper; a friend who always had their hands tucked up their sleeves when you were a teenager; or that bloody woman who kept clicking her pen at a meeting and annoying the hell out of you as you were trying to speak.

Whether we like it or not, we all react to these non-verbal messages. Sometimes we think about them consciously, other times we don't. And just because we aren't *consciously* aware of them doesn't mean that they don't have an effect on us!

Think for a moment about power and status. You walk in to just about any foreign embassy anywhere in the world (if you've not been in one then I'm sure you've seen them in films or on TV). What are you immediately greeted with? Usually the first things you see are the flags. At least one huge flag, if not several, right smack bang in front of you as you enter the building, and then dozens of others of varying sizes dotted around the place. Often you'll see the country's emblem on pictures of beautiful places. You'll see people in smart military uniforms or other security staff.

Then there's other things like security gates, car parking spaces marked for 'Visitors', others marked out especially for the important people who work in the building who may have their own names, initials or titles painted on their space, or, if they're really going for it, their own little etched plastic sign.

Why is all this there?

Simple, it's there to send out a non-verbal message. It's telling you, without it actually needing to be said or written down:

'You are entering officialdom. Enter at your own risk because, once you are inside, we can do anything we like and you know it.

We can choose to grant you a visa, or throw you in jail, or we could just be really nice and give you cups of tea and posh biscuits. We are all-powerful and strong. We are part of the Government.'

OK so I'm exaggerating, but you get the point.

We've grown up with non-verbal messages all throughout our lives.

We learn them from the people we've met, especially from people we view as important to us, or have an influence on our lives: parents, grandparents, siblings, extended family, friends, teachers, sports coaches, Cubs, Brownies, Guides leaders, etc.

We learn as we grow up from all the different people we meet, the situations and circumstances we've been in, and the results of those interactions. Sometimes we take it in at a conscious level, sometimes it's totally unconscious.

Well, guess what?

Your own non-verbal communication is both conscious and unconscious too.

Sometimes you know exactly what you're doing and have free choice. Other times you haven't got a clue, you're not even aware of the signals you're sending out. But just because you're unaware of them, doesn't mean that others haven't picked up on them.

In fact, most of what you do with your body is completely unconscious most of the time. Micro-expressions flash across your face in less than half a second, but that's enough for someone to realize things are not what they seem.

Hopefully, as you read through each chapter, you'll start to notice the world around you more. You'll start to pick up on the non-verbal messages you are exposed to day in and day out. You'll understand that non-verbal communication is not just about physical body movements, signals and gestures. It's all that and much more.

BODY LANGUAGE HAS TAKEN OVER!

Unfortunately, the term 'body language' has become a sweeping term for all non-verbal communication. The problem with this is that most people interpret it as applying only to physical body movements.

You don't hear people say, 'Did you see his/her non-verbal communication?' No, instead they say, 'Did you see his/her body language?' It basically means the same thing, although it's a more limited expression.

Pick up just about any national newspaper when there's a big story on, and somewhere in the column inches you'll find a reference to the person's body language. If not directly, then indirectly:

'They left the Magistrates Court with their heads down to avoid eye contact with the waiting press.'

'She was all smiles as she walked confidently waving to the waiting crowd at the premiere of her new film.'

Non-verbal communication is just as it sounds: an unspoken message that has meaning behind it. By systematically breaking down these types of messages you will learn to read people and situations better, improve the results you achieve and benefit from the ability to decode what is really going on around you.

So from here on in I'm going to be talking about body language but I'll actually be taking its wider definition, and going through all the different elements this covers. There are two main components:

- *Kinesics*: the term anthropologist Ray Birdwhistle first used in 1952 for his studies on how people interact through their body signals, movements and gestures.

- *Proxemics*: a term coined by anthropologist Edward T. Hall back in 1966 referring to the study of distances between people interacting with each other.

By the time you get to the end of this book you'll realize just how much actually comes under the heading 'body language'.

THE THREE MAIN USES OF BODY LANGUAGE

What is all this body language that's going on around us all about? What are its main functions? Well, we use body movements, signals and gestures in three main ways: as code or instruction, as an *emphasizer* and as an *indicator*.

1. Body language as code or instruction

There are certain jobs or circumstances where body language is used to replace words. In situations where verbal communication doesn't work, body movements can be used to relay information to others. Ground crew show the pilot where to go when the plane is taxiing. Bookies at a race course use 'Tic Tac' (their very own secret code which only they and their associates know) to convey changing odds on horses or greyhounds.

Lots of different sports have their own set of body movements that mean something to the initiated and nothing to anyone else. Referees in most sports use hand and arm signals. Some get to wave flags as well.

2.   Body language as an emphasizer

In other situations, body language is used to draw attention to things. A presenter might use their hand and arm like a plane taking off as they mention the growth figures for next year; and many of us use status symbols to emphasize our place in the world. There are all sorts of emphasizers, especially in the brand-conscious business world. Look out for 'things' and items that are intended specifically to impress – from clothing to certificates and accolades, from briefcases to gadgets and gizmos. They're all clues about who you're dealing with and, while they're not absolutes, they are little pieces of the jigsaw that you can use to construct the whole scene.

3.   Body language as an indicator

Body language is like an additional level of commentary that can either confirm or undermine the words being used. You've probably seen people say 'Yes' while shaking their head from side to side indicating 'No'. It works the other way round too – you'll hear the word 'No' accompanied by a nod of the head.

You'll typically see this sort of incongruence between words and body language when people are under pressure to do something they don't really want to do. It's often accompanied by a 'shoulder shrug', which generally indicates one of two things: either 'indecision', being caught between a 'Yes' and a 'No'; or an outright contradiction of the verbal 'Yes'.

INTRODUCING THE YODA SYSTEM

This book concentrates on body language in everyday business situations, starting at 'Hello, how are you?' and taking you all the way through to 'Goodbye'.

I'll cover all the common scenarios and roles we play in our jobs, meetings, presentations and negotiations; in the way we manage, motivate, lead and discipline others. By the time you finish you will have the knowledge and understanding of YODA.

In this case YODA isn't the little green pointy eared character in *Star Wars*. It's a simple approach to understanding what you see, which gives you the opportunity to change things if you want.

● **Y**ou: you have to be fully engaged.

● **O**bserve: just notice things you didn't before.

● **D**ecode: work out what it means.

● **A**dapt: change your behaviour to get better results.

BODY LANGUAGE AT WORK

Body language is pretty universal, with slight variations and meanings depending on the circumstances and culture.

Business in particular has its own culture. Most people act differently in their business lives and their private lives.

One set of behaviours exhibited in a social situation may have a totally different meaning in a business setting.

For instance, you may be sitting back in a chair with the fingers of both hands interlinked behind your head or neck.

If this is you sitting at home late in the evening watching TV then chances are it's a relaxing position as you let the woes of your day wash away.

However, if you're in a business meeting which you think is going well, when the person you're talking to adopts this position, it could be a sign of arrogance.

You

Now I have to say at this point that some people are absolutely awful at reading the signs people send. This can lead to all sorts of problems with relationships, social life and work. Others are just naturally good at picking up on the signals without ever having read a single book or done any training on body language.

Those that are good at reading it are generally the ones that seem to know just how to react or behave in any situation. More often than not, they look comfortable with themselves. People warm to them because they feel at ease in their company. They exude confidence.

Whether you are good at reading body language right now or not, you will understand that *you* are the key to how people react around you. You also have choices about how you react to *them*, but only if you learn to observe more…

Observe

Observation is the starting point for reading body language. Once you can read it, you have choices about what to do with the information.

For instance, if you know someone is lying to you because you've been observing the changes in their body language, you have the choice of calling them out on it, or just tucking that bit of information away for future reference.

If you're oblivious to it then you have no choice, you have to go along with the lie. That could cost you in all sorts of ways: emotionally, financially, even spiritually. Let's face it, no one likes being taken for a mug.

Believe it or not, lying is part of our daily lives. If you say to yourself at this point, 'I don't tell lies', then you are lying to yourself. We all do. Admittedly some are white lies, which are OK because they generally protect someone's feelings, but not all lies have positive intentions.

In business, the truth is not always told and it's sometimes deliberately withheld. For example, in negotiations you don't give away everything up front. You withhold certain information for later.

The more observant you are, the more adept you will be at avoiding pitfalls and understanding when you've pushed a situation to the limit.

Decode

Closely connected to observing is decoding. It's essential that you develop the skills to decode what you are seeing. That way, you stay in control and have the opportunity to choose how to handle a situation.

Decoding starts at the beginning, when you meet someone. That's true whether it's the first meeting or the fifty-first. A person's body language, like their moods and attitudes, changes from moment to moment depending on what's being talked about.

They'll have an opinion on what you are saying. If they like it, their body language will be open, positive and encouraging. But if you suddenly stray onto a tricky subject where you have opposing views, the body language will change in an instant.

I've done experiments on the courses I run, where we've hooked participants up to heart and blood pressure monitors then taken readings while talking about non-controversial subjects. After a while, we've gone into more controversial territory where there's disagreement and, again, we've taken readings.

Surprise, surprise. Heart and blood pressure stay in a nice comfortable relaxed zone when the topics are non-controversial, but introduce any controversy and heart rate and blood pressure rise almost instantly.

What's interesting is that when they're relaxed and comfortable body language is fluid and usually mirrors the other person but as soon as any controversy sneaks in, the body language changes. When asked to try to maintain the mirroring, participants find it extremely difficult and their body movements become more jerky and angular. You might have noticed this in yourself or others.

A quick example is the hand and wrist. When relaxed and fluid the hand rolls loosely at the pivot point of the wrist. This stops the moment someone starts gets more serious about something. At this point, their hand, wrist and forearm begin to move as one, pushing forward with jabbing, sweeping gestures.

If you observe this, you are in a position to decode it and make sense of it. In this situation, a sudden rigidity in someone's gestures will tell you that whatever has just been said or done prior to the change is important to that person. With this insight into their thoughts, you then have the option either to go back and cover it in a different way or change the subject completely and talk about something less important or controversial.

If you want to see this change in action watch TV programmes like *Question Time*, *Prime Minister's Question Time*, *The Apprentice* or any other show that features people with opposing views. One minute they'll be all relaxed and fluid and the next they're stiff and rigid.

Adapt

You will have picked up by now that the greatest gift to come from understanding someone through their body language is that it gives you choices.

It gives insight into how they are feeling at any moment. Once you've learned to tap into someone's emotions, you can build a much deeper level of trust and rapport with them. In business, that means people are more likely to enjoy working with you.

- Adapting can only be done if you observe and decode first.

- Adapting can bring surprising results very quickly.

- Adapting is your free choice.

But what exactly is adapting? Adapting means changing your default reaction to something more consciously designed to shift the other person from their position to a different one – one that is better for you.

YODA IN A NUTSHELL

YODA is a simple system that covers reading, interpreting and acting on body language cues – both that you spot around you, and that you display yourself.

You

- You need to be fully aware that the signals you give off will have an effect on others.
- You need to understand that your moods affect the signals you give out and, in turn, receive.

Observe

- You will already be observing body language at some level depending on your innate awareness of it.
- Start looking deeper at smaller details you may have been missing to expand your knowledge.

Decode

- Decoding gives you choices about how to handle different individuals and different situations.

Adapt

- When you've mastered body language you will be able to adapt the signals you send out yourself, and your responses to other people's body language.

- Empower yourself by increasing your range of options in different situations.

Mastering body language can literally transform relationships:

- You're more in tune with everyone around you.
- You become the one that everyone likes to be around.
- You become the one people trust.
- You become the person other people recommend to their business colleagues.

Why?

Simple. If you can adapt it shows flexibility. It means you have the personality to get on better with a wide range of people. This is a key skill in every walk of life, because we live and work in a rapidly changing world.

We do this all the time, in most cases without realizing that we've already been through the process of observing and decoding a set of signals to get there.

Here's a really simple example. Let's say two guys are standing face to face talking about football and one is winding the other up about the results the previous Saturday. The butt of the jokes starts to get annoyed and their body language changes: eyes glare, teeth become gritted, shoulders are tensed and fists clench. It's a physical reaction which says, 'Don't push me or I'm going to explode'.

If you've noticed it, which you almost certainly would because that particular set of signals spells danger, you have a choice right there and then, whether to keep pushing their buttons or back off. Unless you want them to vent their anger you'd be a fool to keep pushing. Sometimes in a fight it's better just to back down.

That's the adapting part. This is an extreme example, but as you can see, it's not rocket science. It's what we do automatically.

This book is all about making you more aware of opportunities to adapt, through your observation and decoding skills.

SUMMARY

In brief, this book will give you a thorough understanding of the importance of body language in the workplace, but it will help in every area of your life.

It will help you see the body language behind your interactions with others, and this insight in turn will give you many more choices in how you engage with and react to people.

You will learn how to change and adapt your own body language to give you more confidence when you need it.

You'll learn how to play with body language to discover what works best for you.

You'll learn about the gaps in our minds and the unconscious effect non-verbal communication has on us all.

You will also learn the answers to two of the most common questions I'm asked when training people or giving speeches.

'How do you know when someone is physically attracted to you?'

and

'How do you know when someone is lying to you?'

Yes, this book focuses on body language in business situations, but everyone wants to know if someone finds them attractive! It's part of human nature. It's part of the future survival of the human race. Maybe it's something you could use in your next negotiation too.

When one person finds another attractive, there's a whole set of common signals they both display. Lots of relationships start through business interactions, and this can be both an advantage and a disadvantage. You need to know what to look out for.

The same can be said for lying. Everyone would love to know when they're being sold a lie. After all, honesty is one of the basic building blocks of relationships. When it breaks down and the trust goes, the relationship is generally doomed. It doesn't matter if it's a friendship or a business relationship, there has to be a certain level of trust between people.

Understanding body language will help you build trust and rapport. It will certainly give you more choices, which will empower you, in every area of your life.

2

THE SCIENCE OF BODY LANGUAGE

THE BRAIN BODY CONNECTION

The science behind body language is centred on your feelings, attitudes and emotions to internal and external stimuli.

Internal thoughts feed into external behaviour. Think about something sad for long enough and your body language changes to reflect your thoughts, even if only slightly.

EXERCISE

Assuming you're in an appropriate place, try this right now. Stand up, in front of a mirror if possible, and just pretend for a moment you're at a concert of your favourite band or singer, or are celebrating some major sporting victory. Put a great big smile on your face, throw your arms up in the air like you just don't care, and play the part of being as happy as you can ever remember being. Then freeze frame it. Take a note, both mentally and physically, of your body language – your facial expression, how your body feels.

Now switch your thoughts to something sad like losing a pet, the break-up of a relationship or anything that makes you feel miserable.

Here's the hard part. Try to keep your body language and facial expressions exactly the same as in the first part of the exercise, when you were happy. You should find it virtually impossible.

When I've tried this experiment with groups it is extremely rare that anyone can maintain the same body language. Even if there are only small changes, it should prove to you that your internal thoughts, the words you use to talk to yourself, the pictures in your head, the memories, all project onto your body.

The key to understanding body language is to be aware that we all express our internal thoughts *externally,* through our body movements, signals, gestures and facial expressions.

As I mentioned very briefly earlier, most body language is unconscious. We just react to stimuli, whether they are internal or external.

Once you understand that, for the most part, people just react without thinking, it gives you the opportunity to observe the actions, decode them, and adapt.

HOW THE BRAIN PROCESSES INFORMATION

The brain is an incredible piece of computing technology housed inside something not a lot bigger than a coconut shell.

> 'The brain processes 400 billion bits of information a second. BUT, we are ONLY aware of 2,000 of those.'

> Dr. Joseph Dispenza, D.C.

However, it doesn't need all that information, so it deletes most of it and just keeps what it thinks are the important bits.

Right now as you're reading this are you aware of:

● The temperature?

● The sounds around you?

● The clothes touching your skin?

● The voice in your head that is reading these words?

● The feelings of your feet inside your shoes, socks, slippers?

● The texture or weight of the book or device you are holding?

● The smells around you, even your own smell?

The answer for most people is a resounding 'No'. But here's the interesting bit. As you read each question in the list above, your brain would have become aware of each of those things in turn, and in most cases it will have gone to check on them.

Did it?

If it did, then great. You are now aware that there's a lot more going on than you thought. Knowing this gives you a new understanding of how your brain processes information.

If you read those questions and answered 'No', your brain didn't go and check, even for a split second, then you are probably one of those people who is just oblivious to what their body is doing most of the time. Don't worry. In that case, this book will be even more useful to you. It will make you more aware of everything going on around you and how you can make the most of it.

Making sense of it

Now, I should say at this point, that I am a fully registered hypnotherapist and NLP (neuro linguistic programming) trainer, and part of what I just did with you above is commonly used in hypnosis and NLP.

It's a way of controlling the general direction of someone's thought processes by utilizing their own senses. It's how we encode our experiences in this world. There is nothing more powerful than your senses: seeing, hearing, feeling, smelling and tasting.

Or, as they prefer to call it in NLP: VAKOG – visual, auditory, kinaesthetic, olfactory, gustatory.

VAKOG is a way of breaking down a person's thinking into the five senses, based on the verbal language you hear them use. In essence, the idea is that what you hear a person say, tells you what sense they are using to process the thinking behind it, whether it's visual, auditory, kinaesthetic, olfactory or gustatory. Or if you prefer see, hear, touch, smell and taste (SHTST makes about as much sense as VAKOG!).

If you think about a holiday you've been on when you were sitting by the pool sipping your favourite drink, then you will most likely have pictures of part or all of the scene come up in your head. In this instance you are using your visual memory.

How it works

Listen to any conversation and within every two or three sentences you will hear words that use one of the senses.

Visual

'See what I mean?'

'What's your perspective?'

'Can you see it from my point of view?'

'I'm a big picture person, I've got a vision for this company and the outlook is good.'

Auditory

'How does that sound to you?'

'Do you like what you're hearing?'

'I hear what you're saying.'

'We're singing from same song sheet and in tune as a team.'

Kinaesthetic

'OK so how do you feel about that?'

'Can we just touch on how we handle this problem better in the future?'

'We need to strike and balance or it will just be too painful.'

'It makes me feel numb at the thought of it'

EXERCISE

The next time you speak to someone, listen to what sense is being used. Which sense do they relate to most often? Once you have that information, simply feed all your information back to them using the same sense. For example:

- **Client:** 'We see ourselves as growing fast over the next two years.'

- **You:** 'That's great. Can you paint me a picture of where you see yourself going?'
- **Manager**: I'm hearing good things about your new project.'
- **You:** 'Good. All the feedback so far is sounding very positive.'
- **Union Rep:** 'The Union feels that the new shift schedule is unworkable.'
- **You:** 'Well that leaves me numb. Tell more about why they feel that way?'

It's a very simple system really. You just listen to the words being used. All very interesting, but how does this fit in with body language. As I said, there's a body language component to representational systems as well.

Visual

- Visual people tend to breathe with just the top of their lungs so their breaths are short. Just watch the chest or notice how long they take between talking and breathing.

- They also have a tendency to keep their body and head straight and upright, leaning in towards other people. They remember in pictures or videos they can see in their heads.

- They are usually very organized, ordered and tidy.

- They are most often of thin or slim build.

- It's how things look that is important to visual people.

Auditory

- Auditory people have a tendency to breathe lower down in the middle of their chest.

- They'll move their eyes sideways when thinking about things and you'll often see them either using their lips while they talk internally or just plain talk to themselves out loud.

- They remember things by repeating them verbally in sequences.

- They are often interested in music and very talkative. They love chatting on the phone rather than email.

- What others say about them is important.

Kinaesthetic

- Kinaesthetic people breathe way down using their diaphragm so you see their belly move up and down with the chest. Their breathing is longer and slower and consequently their speech is slower, as are their general body movements.

- They prefer to remember by acting things out in their minds or even physically.

- It is how others feel about them that is important to them.

USING VAKOG

Representational systems can be a useful tool for learning about different types of people, but don't be fooled into thinking that everyone fits a profile or sticks to just one sense.

They don't. It constantly shifts from one to the other and back again then to a different one. Some people just cannot be pigeonholed.

However, most people do have a dominant representational system followed by a secondary one and will switch from one to another. Just listen carefully and go with the two most commonly used senses or, alternatively, be flexible and mirror back without trying to uncover a predominant system:

- **Client**: 'We see our company moving into ...... sector.'
- **You**: 'Do you see it as a big market?'
- **Client**: 'We feel it has mass potential.'
- **You**: 'Can you flesh that out a little more?'
- **Client**: 'Well, we heard that ...... is pulling out of that sector.'
- **You**: 'Well that sounds good. Tell me more.'

The other two, olfactory and gustatory aren't that useful because most people don't process information through their noses or tongues. You do hear people talk using those senses, however.

- **Olfactory:** 'Everything you've told me stinks of bullshit!'

- **Gustatory:** 'I can just taste the money already!'

VAKOG is just one area of NLP. If what you've read has sparked a feeling of interest and it sounds like a good idea to learn more, go delve deeper into this touching area of human behaviour research and see where it takes you. How does that sound? As with all other areas I will be covering, please don't try to run before you can walk. Practise with friends, family, good work colleagues – and complete strangers.

When I say complete strangers I don't mean just go up to people on the street. I mean people you meet in a bar, in the queue for a bus, or a waiting room. Use the chance encounters that happen all the time.

It's also important to bear in mind that we actually have many more than five senses. Some are subdivisions of the main five, but there are others that are completely separate. We have a sense of balance, pressure, hot, cold, pain, hunger, movement, location, direction, proximity. One study I looked at in the *New Scientist* showed some 21 senses or more. All of them come into play when it comes to body language because we not only encode our experiences through these senses, we also have an effect on others with those same senses.

If you fart loudly in a crowded lift, do you think that it will have an effect on the other people in there with you? Of course it will, because apart from not being an acceptable thing to do in company, especially stuck in a lift, your mind is programmed to associate the noise with a smell that is generally unpleasant.

Your brain makes associations based on your previous experiences or programming and this affects your observation skills as well.

OBSERVATION SKILLS

If you're with me so far, you'll understand that the way you were brought up, the way you've lived your life and all your experiences to date, determine how you observe the world and people around you.

People who've grown up in a safe, secure and happy environment are generally more trusting and less suspicious of others, while those who've had a tough childhood are often less trusting and more fearful. This tends to make them more observant and more aware of things that might hurt them.

Your observation skills are affected by many things, from your moods, thoughts and attitudes to your life experiences.

If you trust someone implicitly, you don't even look for suspicious behaviour. On the other hand, if you really don't trust someone you will be on the lookout for anything that will prove your suspicions to be correct.

Sometimes you'll form an instant like or dislike for someone you've only just met, and stick with your opinion even if other information contradicts it.

If a friend talks about another friend you've never met, by the time you do you'll already have heard little snippets and stories about them, influencing your judgement and causing you to look for supporting evidence.

We actively look for supporting evidence to prop up our opinions and ignore just about everything that doesn't fit with them. But

your brain can only be truly observant when it judges people, situations and circumstances with little or no preconceived ideas. If you've already been influenced, you can't look at things with an open mind.

LEFT AND RIGHT BRAIN

The different sides of the brain process information differently. The brain is split into two hemispheres, one on the left side controlling the right side of the body, one on the right controlling the left. The connecting bit in between is called the corpus callosum, and it allows the two sides to communicate faster than the fastest broadband. Each side processes different sorts of information. They act together and independently at the same time.

In 1981 Dr Roger Sperry, a Noble prize winner, had a patient suffering from uncontrollable seizures. He removed a small section of the corpus callosum and later, when testing the patient, he could isolate one side of the brain and body from the other.

In one test, the patient was given an object to look at or feel whilst one side of their brain was isolated, meaning that the information the brain was receiving was incomplete. The result was an astonishing demonstration of how the two sides of the brain differ in their roles.

Results showed that the left brain could identify what the object was, a pen for instance, but not what you did with it. The right brain on the other hand knew exactly what to do with the object but not what it was.

This was the first time it had been clearly demonstrated that the two sides of the brain process information differently.

There have been lots of studies on left and right brain function and they all pretty much come to the same conclusions. Here's a brief list of what each is responsible for.

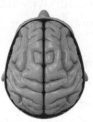

Left brain	Right brain
Logical/analytical	Emotional/feeling
Language/words	Symbolic/visual
Linear/ordered	Abstract/big picture

So what's all this got to do with body language? As you'll see later, when we cover 'eye accessing cues', understanding that we interpret different information in separate sides of the brain can give you an additional level of insight into the mind of the person you're dealing with. If you've mastered body language, you can literally *see* how someone is thinking.

In a lot of business environments more emphasis is put on left-brain, logical, analytical, ordered, reasoning functions, than it is on the creative, intuitive, abstract right brain. This is not really surprising. It follows most people's school experiences where we are taught to prioritize maths, English, history, physics, biology and chemistry, over sport, music, drama and art. Really only a fraction of our time in education is dedicated to right-brain activities.

Even if you were once creative, as with most pre-school children, by the time you're aged around 7 years old your creativity will have been stifled by the left brain dominated world of education. After that, it drops off significantly.

Studies have shown that by that age, less than 10% of children are still highly creative and this drops to just 2% of the overall population by the time we're adults.

This is at least part of the reason why in business we tend to forget the human side and concentrate on facts, figures and deadlines.

Because business is so institutionalized, it's easy to forget that you're dealing with other human beings, who respond better if you become better at understanding them and their emotional states. Appealing to both the logical left brain and the emotional, free thinking right is a powerful skill.

CONSCIOUS AND UNCONSCIOUS

Earlier I mentioned that we do some things on purpose and are in full conscious control, while other times we do things and we're completely unconscious and oblivious to them.

Knowing what's conscious and unconscious will help you immensely in decoding signals. That's the key to this section. Anything that is unconscious means it is happening without interference by the conscious mind. The mind can only react and respond instinctively in these situations. Conscious things on the other hand, like a presentation or meeting, can be pre-planned. In these situations, you can dictate exactly where you want to sit or stand, what you wear and what you want around yourself to create the best impact and impression.

These things are used all the time in business to create a brand image, so be warned. Consciously we can be quite easily fooled, unconsciously we cannot.

So what are the unconscious things we do?

Blinking, blushing, sweating, self-touching, scratching, pupil dilation and constriction, muscle tone, micro and macro facial expressions, shoulder shrugs, eyebrow movements, breathing and numerous other things – not forgetting picking your nose in the car!

Each of these areas will be covered in context later in the book (well maybe I'll miss out the picking your nose bit) to give you a fuller understanding of just how unconscious behaviour operates.

Basically most of what we do is a habit pattern learned over years and years. We feel comfortable with our habits. They are the unconscious actions that dictate what you do with your body, day in and day out. It starts first thing in the morning when you wake up and continues throughout your day, unless something makes you change it.

Here's a typical habit pattern for most people.

- Alarm goes off

- Go to bathroom

- Make tea/coffee/breakfast

- Back to bathroom for shower/bath

- Dry off

- Get dressed

- Head off to work.

That might not be your exact morning sequence but it'll be along similar lines. It's an unconscious habit pattern. Within those headline actions, each has its own set of habits that you've developed to make your life easier.

When the alarm goes off, you either snooze or you get up straight away. Chances are you do the same thing every working day with maybe a change at the weekend.

When you make tea/coffee/breakfast, you'll probably have the same drink every morning, unless you've run out, and then you change and have whatever is left or nothing. You're either one of those who waits for the kettle to boil or does other things while it's boiling. Still an unconscious habit if you do it the same every day.

Your shower or bath ritual probably follows the same pattern every time with the odd change here and there, and you'll more than likely dry yourself in the same sequence every time too.

When you get dressed, nine times out of ten, you put your left/right leg or arm into your clothing first and you probably don't even realize it.

If you want to see just how ingrained your set of habits is, tomorrow morning be very aware of the order you do things and notice how your body tells you what is normal. Then just try to do the opposite. I guarantee that within 30 minutes you'll have driven yourself nuts and you'll be desperate to slip back into the old, easy, unconscious habits.

The point that I'm making here is that it's not just your morning ritual that has these habit patterns. You have them in every area of your daily life, you just don't realize it. In fact, most of what you do with your body every day is 95% the same.

With your emotions, if you're feeling happy, you'll have a pattern of happiness signals. If you're feeling sad, you'll have a set of sadness signals. The same can be said for all the emotions, attitudes and feelings you express through your body. They all have a set of movements, signals and gestures that are pretty much identical from one day to the next.

This is neither good nor bad, it just means you have a set of signals that anyone can observe and decode about how you are feeling at any point throughout the day. And, likewise, you can tune into other people's unconscious body language.

You know on a Monday morning how people's weekends have gone – and you don't need to hear what they're saying to pick up on whether they've been good or not. Some body language is very clear and universal. Some is more unique to them, based on their unconscious habits. You have to start consciously noticing it all, and that starts with the patterns in people's behaviour that tell you how they're feeling.

SUMMARY

This chapter has shown you that your body language is based on the feedback your brain receives from both internal and external stimuli. That feedback is based on your senses and how your brain perceives a situation, which in turn comes from your own observational skills.

Then there is the role the two hemispheres of your brain play in being able to determine certain information and how you are influenced in your day-to-day decision making by both your conscious thoughts and the unconscious sensory perceptions.

But it doesn't stop with the physical body movements, signals and gestures, it's much bigger than that, as you're about to find out.

3

WHY BODY LANGUAGE IS BIGGER THAN YOU THINK

THE WAY WE DRESS

Body language is the term that's been adopted for all things non-verbal but it's misleading. Non-verbal communication means everything, right down to the way you dress. If you wear a uniform there's not usually much in the way of personalization, but you can see it if you look.

As a teenager I remember vividly two of my local bus conductors from the days when the driver was locked away at the front of the bus and you had a conductor collecting the fairs and calling out each stop along the route.

Both these conductors wore the standard grey uniform jacket, trousers and peaked cap of the bus company. The only difference was that one had badges all over his jacket lapels and the other had badges all over his cap. Each of these little badges meant something to them. They wanted people to see them, and if you asked, they would happily tell you a story of how they came to get each of them. They were the Pearly Kings of bus conductors.

It was a way of personalizing the 'standard'. They didn't want to be seen as a clone, in the plain old bus company uniform. They wanted people to see them as different, as individuals.

Even if you don't have a uniform and you can choose what you wear every day, people on the whole conform to their industry standard.

In banking it's probably suits. So you wear one, but you choose the style and cut. You'll buy different shirt/blouse and tie combinations and you'll have specific jewellery or make-up to go with them. You might even wear badges like Rotary Club or a Blood Donor Heart.

If you are in the design or fashion world you'll probably have complete freedom of choice and be as individual as possible, but you'll still fit with your industry norms. No matter how way out you go, you're conforming to a certain extent.

Clothing and the way we dress is a big area of personalization and it sends our strong messages. So look at what people wear and consider the following:

- Does it all fit properly? If not, why not? Is it just their physical size? i.e. very short, tall, thin, thick. Is it harder to find clothing?

- Does it fit their role?

- Do they look the part?

- Is it clean and pressed?

- Is it cheap or expensive?

- Is anything out of place?

- What message are they trying to send?

- What message are you actually receiving?

As the old saying goes: *If it walks, swims and quacks like a duck, it probably is a duck.*

If you see a business woman all dressed up in a good-quality suit, expensive jewellery and perfectly coiffured hair and make-up, who also happens to be wearing several raggedy old friendship bands round their wrists, you have to ask yourself, where does that fit into this personality?

It's often the simplest of things that give away the most. To me, this would indicate someone who is comfortable and confident that they can be professional and on the ball, but that they also have an emotional side and they're not frightened to show it.

Personally, I'd make a point of bringing up the bands in conversation because then I can make an emotional connection with them, and that builds rapport. That's your choice depending on how brave you are and whether you even want to get to a deeper level with them.

Bear in mind that we all have different personalities depending on the situation we're in. Most of us act differently with fellow workers to the way we do with our own families, our children and friends. We generally encounter each of these groups of people in different environments, so let's take a look at that area next.

ENVIRONMENT – HOME, TRANSPORT AND WORK

The environment plays a major role in how we feel. It might be the people in a particular place or the buildings themselves. Often there is a link between the people and the building. It can make us feel comfortable and relaxed or uncomfortable and stressed, and all without us even realizing it.

Walk into any court of law in the land and you'll see people with long faces, biting their nails, fidgeting, pacing up and down, crying. The building and the people in it, its layout and design, all influence and add to the emotional states felt by the people inside. You'll typically see Her Majesty's Crown emblems and carvings on the walls, security staff, uniformed police, legal teams dressed in cloaks and wigs, clerks with clipboards. There are symbols of power and authority everywhere you look. Even if it's not you in the dock you'll still feel the emotions of those who are, their relatives and any victims waiting for justice to be done.

Shopping centres, supermarkets, cinemas and theme parks are designed to control the flow of people traffic, as they move past all the restaurants, coffee shops and toilets strategically placed along the way. Even the lighting, music and temperature are nicely controlled for us – all to keep us in a happy-go-lucky mood and to encourage us to spend money.

Next time you go to a big shopping centre see if you can spot a clock anywhere. Chances are you won't. They don't want you thinking about time. They want you to stick around without worrying about it. If you spot the time, you might suddenly rush off and stop spending money.

Every environment has its purpose. For the most part, the way it's laid out is out of your hands, but there are three areas where we have lots of influence, and total control in some instances: travel, home and work.

These three areas also just happen to be where most of us spend most of our time, so there's usually lots of valuable information there just waiting to be observed. You see, whenever and wherever people have to spend time, they'll usually find ways to make it more comfortable. Makes sense really – you don't want to spend hours in car, home or office if you don't like it. If you have any choice over how it looks, what's in it and how it makes you feel, you'll more than likely choose to make it as comfortable as possible.

And it's these little comfort signs that tell us things about the people who inhabit the spaces. Sometimes you discover things that you would never know otherwise, just from observing and decoding the objects that someone has added to their space of their own free will. Making these observations about someone's environment and what they've chosen to put in it can completely change the way you interact with them.

I remember back in 1998 I had a meeting with this guy who was at the top of his game handling the magazines and brochures for the big stores. He had a nice plush office situated at the top of one of the tallest buildings in Bristol city centre. My colleague and I entered his office and we were immediately hit by the fact that this guy had the most enormous collection of snow globes you've ever seen in your life (outside the snow globe museum, that is). They were all lined up neatly along the low window ledge, maybe two or three hundred of them. On the walls there were certificates and magazine awards.

He had the big desk, a high-back leather chair that swivelled in every direction, rocked back and forth with padded arm and head rests. My colleague and I were given two standard, four-legged, cloth-padded, static chairs with no arm rests – you know the sort.

Now if you happen to be a boss or manager reading this and you have your own office, please take note. This type of set-up is not conducive to doing business with anyone apart from a particular group of people. It's fine if you really want to say to everyone who enters, 'Look at my globes. Go on, ask me about them. And the certificates and the awards. Go on, ask me. Oh and by the way, sit down there in that little standard office chair while I look down on you from my superior super-duper executive chair.'

Now I'm not saying don't do it, just that you should consider whether your office is sending out the right signals. Is it inviting and friendly, a place to do business and manage staff?

In the sales industry it is commonplace to put emphasis on things like achievement, status and wealth, so you will see awards, certificates and displays of success all around. Not everyone is motivated by such things though. In fact some people are turned off by it.

Offices, like people's cars and homes, are a mine of useful information, revealing their occupants' likes and even dislikes. I've seen 'No Smoking' signs in all three environments. An office you can understand, it's the law. But in your car or home? Whoever put it there didn't need to, but they chose to in order to tell the world, 'I don't want smoking here, thank you very much.'

Let's take an in-depth look at each environment in turn.

Transport

Obviously a car, van, lorry or bicycle are more personal than public transport but, however you travel, you take things with you to make the journey more comfortable, bearable and interesting.

People who use their vehicles for work, like a sales or trades person with tools or supplies, will personalize it even more because of the amount of time they spend in it.

What to observe in a vehicle

In exactly the same way you go about observing the way people dress, you have to look out for two main things: either things that go together or things that simply don't. You are looking for things that confirm or conflict with the overall impression, as with the example of the business woman earlier, whose wrist bands conflicted with her smart suit.

If you're bold enough, have a nose in the glove box or centre console. Look above the sun visors and inside the door pockets. Even if you don't want to turn yourself into a CSI agent there's still enough to observe. Here are some pointers:

● Look at things hanging from the rear view mirror, on the dashboard or parcel shelves.

- Are there any religious symbols, lucky charms, photos, fluffy creatures?

- Musical tastes are quite often on display – is it one genre or an eclectic mix of old and new?

- If it's on, what radio station is it tuned to – news, local, music?

- Are there any books around? What genre? Business, self-development, fiction, biography?

- Do they have a personalized number plate? Does it spell a name? Is it an old or new car?

- Are there any stickers on the windows or bumpers? What are they? Political, sport, clubs?

- Can you see kiddie seats, organizers or DVD players on the head restraints?

- Take a look in the ashtray. Are they a smoker or non smoker? (Have they got a little sign?)

- How clean is it inside and out? If it needs a clean how long has it needed it?

You get the idea. There's so much you can observe even in the small space of a car. So what's the point of noticing all these things anyway? Well, they're reference points. They give you choice. They are conversation starters if ever you need them and they are clues to the driver's personality.

You'll never know everything about a person but all these little observations will help you to understand a lot more about them.

Look around and fill in some gaps about their likes and dislikes. The knowledge will come in handy in all sorts of ways. You can choose to talk about the things you've noticed to find out more, or you can just store it away for future reference. You can use this information to confirm or change your opinions about them.

Other vehicles

Even if someone doesn't have a car they'll travel by bus, train or bike. They too will have things they carry with them to make their journey as nice as possible. It'll be stashed away in backpacks, briefcases, handbags and laptops.

Now I'm not for one minute suggesting you go nosing around in someone's bag, unless you're very brave, stupid or know the person extremely well. You don't have to go diving into these things to see what people carry in them. People arrive at their place of work every day all over the country with these portable storage vessels, then go and empty the contents out for everyone to see: mobile phones, game consoles, laptops, purses, wallets, keys, footwear, even a full change of clothing. People carry absolutely all sorts of things designed to make life easier, better. What do you carry around and what does it say about you?

EXERCISE

Simply empty out your handbag, briefcase, rucksack or whatever else you use to carry your personal belongings around and see what information the contents reveal about you.

Home

As the saying goes; *'A man's home is his castle'.* Home is generally a place of refuge, safety and comfort, no matter how big or small. Even if you don't like where you live, you'll do your best to make it as nice as possible for the time you do have to spend there.

Your home is full of information. Your home is a blank slate you can play with and style in a way that suits you. More so than your car, it is up to you to decide who gets invited in, and who doesn't. How would you feel at the thought of your boss, new girlfriend/boyfriend or prospective in-laws just turning up at to your home unannounced?

Your home is a place to relax and be yourself, and that's exactly why it can completely contradict the outward impression you've built up.

Be honest – when did you last clean the bathroom? Get rid of the cobwebs? Run the vacuum round? Pick up all the dirty washing? Tidy the kids' toys? Put all your DVDs back in their cases?

If you're at home reading this, take a good look round and see what's displayed that you wouldn't want everyone in your life to see. I can guarantee you've got things you wouldn't want to share. I can also guarantee that hidden away around the house you've got even more private stuff. Everyone has things from their past or present interests that they'd rather keep to themselves. It might be a passion for ballroom dancing and science fiction movies or it might be something more private.

What to observe in the home

The dumping ground for most people when they get home is right after you walk through the door. You find all sorts of clues on the porch, in the entrance hall and on the stairs. Yes, all the normal things like shoes, coats, hats and scarves, which in the case of a family will give you a rough idea of age, sex and how many people live in the house, but you'll also see other things that will tell you more about the person or family. Look for kids' toys, sports equipment, bikes, photos or art on the walls.

Go into any room and you'll find lots and lots of hints about the owner's likes and dislikes. Photographs are very personal, so if there are any on show, see if there's theme. Are they of family, achievement awards, sports, friends, arty stuff or a mix of all of them? Take a look on bookshelves – what sort of books are there? Do they follow a theme? Newspapers and magazines give you clues about political persuasions and hobbies. You're not being nosy looking at all these things. They're on show. You're just noticing what's there.

Work

The work environment is a little different to the first two. People:

1.   Don't always have total control over it.

2.   Don't often share too much personal stuff.

3.   Don't tend to be totally themselves at work.

Whether you have your very own office, a small cubicle in an open-plan office or work in a warehouse, you will have *some* control over your personal space. The difference in the way office space is personalized is that it generally ends up being a mix of personal and work-related possessions.

If you are lucky enough to have your very own office and have had free choice over its layout, décor, furnishings and everything else, then take a look at what impression you are setting for your visitors.

- What's on display for people to see? Does it fit your position? Does it set the right tone for the majority of meetings you have?

- How's the seating arranged? Is your chair big and the others small?

- What's on the desk? Is it simply a keyboard and monitor screen or all manner of other bits and bobs like a personal organizer, desk tidy, files, folders, photos and things the kids have made?

- What's on the walls, in display cabinets and written on whiteboards? People often forget things they put on whiteboards and flip charts!

- Does it smell nice? People often don't realize that if they spend all day in their office, it's going to smell of them. Our sense of smell is one of the most basic but sensitive of all our senses, so certain types of smells resonate within us at a very deep and primal level. Research shows we can recognize the smell of our mother within minutes of being born. Our sense of smell can warn us of bad things, like when your milk goes off! Its design has a built-in danger detector. Start to notice when your sense of smell flags something unpleasant to you. It's a natural warning.

What do other people's offices say to you? What personal information can you glean from them?

I recommend that clients who have the freedom and space should have two differently designed meeting rooms. One for the soft, friendly, open meetings where you want to woo clients, persuade staff and gain cooperation. Another with a harsher design, layout and lighting, for the hardball meetings where you need to discipline staff or deal with serious matters.

The *Big Brother* TV series played around with all sorts of different designs and got different reactions from the 'inmates' to different environments, whether it was taking out frustrations, or abusing completely inanimate objects. People do this in offices too. Everyone kicks the photocopier at some point!

Work environments quite often have a specific corporate image that limits options for personalization, but people find a way, even if it's just their own coffee cup from home. Corporate culture also plays a part. Environment and culture go 'hand in hand' or 'hand in glove' (two more everyday expressions related to body parts used to express that certain things just go together). So, let's now take a look at culture itself.

CULTURE AND BODY LANGUAGE

Culture is as big as a country or as small as a group. It influences your body language immensely, although in reality it is nothing more than a set of learned behaviour responses to what is considered the norm in different situations.

Culture can be vastly different, as in the difference between how a person from one country expresses simple things like 'Yes' and 'No'. People in most of the world nod the head up and down for 'Yes' and shake it from side to side for 'No', but it's not the same everywhere. In fact it's the complete opposite in parts of Bulgaria, Turkey, Iran and a few other countries. There, a flick of the head upward accompanied by a verbal 'Tsk' or 'Tut' means 'No' and a shake of the head side to side to means 'Yes'. Confusing.

Just imagine for second that you're with someone who does everything the opposite way to you. Try to *say* 'Yes' while shaking your head, then say 'No' while nodding your head. It really is quite hard.

There are plenty of other countries too, where a simple yes or no could get you in trouble if you don't know the cultural differences and get it wrong.

Incidentally, the norm for nodding the head for yes in the UK can actually take several forms. There's the single nod for simple acknowledgement of information exchanged and understood. Then there's the double nod, which signifies definite agreement. The triple nod shows someone is agreeing and thinking something over. Four nods or more and you just look like a confused lunatic! Go ahead and try it. Just keep nodding when you're next talking with someone and watch their facial expression. You'll normally see them raise one eyebrow, which is a sign of confusion. It says 'What?'

Cultural confusion comes in lots of forms. Hitch-hiking with your thumb up in the air pushing forward in the direction you wish to

travel could quite easily get you beaten up in some countries. It's basically an insult: you're saying, 'Up yours driver!'

The thumbs-up gesture is quite common all around the world but the meanings attached to it are wide and various;

- It's the international diving signal for up.

- It means good, OK and yes.

- It means the number one, (or sometimes the number five).

- It can mean 'We have a deal' as in using the thumb on a wax seal.

- It's an insult.

So if you're doing business with someone from another country, be careful.

SHOW ME THE MONEY

There's a commonly used hand signal where the tip of the index finger curls inward to meet the tip of the thumb. It's often referred to as the OK sign, and just like the thumbs up, it has many different meanings, one of which is 'money' in Japan. If you used this sign as you said something like, 'That's all fine when can we sign the paperwork?', it could be interpreted as, 'I'd like some bribe money before signing any paperwork'.

Body language across cultures is big news. I've given two examples here just to give you a taste, but there are whole books dedicated to it. Even some travel guides now include sections on the meanings of certain signals and gestures to assist travellers.

On a smaller scale, a company can have its own culture, and certain jobs within an organization can have their very own set of body language signals that go along with it.

Airline stewards demonstrating the flight safety procedure run through a whole host of body movements that are more or less exactly the same every single time they do it. A police officer directing traffic uses specific signals to tell the motorist what to do. You see goal-scoring rituals every Saturday and Sunday on every football pitch in the land, sometimes with each player having his or her own role routine within it.

Just about every form of group has its own culture and the smaller the group, the less likely anyone outside that particular group

PUTTING YOUR FOOT DOWN

A very common mistake for travellers to certain parts of the Middle East, Asia and Africa, is showing or pointing to the soles of the feet.

The sole of the foot is considered to be dirty in these cultures because it makes contact with the ground. Sitting with your legs crossed at the knees, kicking back and crossing your feet at the ankles or even sitting in what's called the figure four leg position, is considered extremely rude as it exposes the sole of the foot, which generally ends up pointing at someone, therefore insulting them inadvertently.

is to understand it. Some groups deliberately keep their particular signals secret, like the Masons who are said to have special handshakes.

If you don't know the rules of a particular culture you could make lots of mistakes. Getting it wrong could, at the very least, lead to an embarrassing moment at a business meeting. At the very worst, it could get you killed. That's a bold statement, so here's how someone who should have known better nearly caused the death of some American students who ended up in Iraq when they shouldn't have been, getting themselves thrown in jail.

In his book *The Do's and Taboos of Body Language Around the World*, Roger Axtell recalls how Congressman Bill Richardson unknowingly sat down and crossed his legs at a meeting with Saddam Hussein, pointing the sole of his foot straight at Saddam, who immediately got up and left the room without saying a word. Luckily, after the cultural mistake had been explained, he returned and the Congressman ended up securing the students' freedom.

Someone of a Congressman's standing, flying halfway round the world to Baghdad trying to negotiate the freedom of fellow Americans, either should have known better or, at the very least, been briefed by staff that did!

The same can be said of you if you're doing business in foreign countries. Don't make simple but costly mistakes. Find out about local customs. You'll never know all of them, but at least by knowing the basics, you won't embarrass yourself or spoil a deal.

SUMMARY

This chapter has shown you that it is not just physical movements that count. The way you dress has a major influence, both over how you feel in yourself and how others feel about you.

Your surroundings also play a role in how you conduct yourself. You'll be different down the pub with your work colleagues to the way you are in work with those same people. Surroundings have the ability to relax, excite or intimidate people.

The same can be said of different cultures: if you understand them you can feel quite relaxed, but if you don't they have the power to intimidate or confuse and that will change your body language...

Wherever you go, foreign lands or here at home, almost every face-to-face human interaction starts with a greeting of one form or another.

PART TWO

4

GREETINGS

IT ALL STARTS WITH 'HELLO'

Observing physical body language starts from the moment you say 'hello'. If you don't start then, you'll have no real basis for drawing any conclusions later. If you don't start with 'hello' you'll only be taking snap shots of different parts of the interaction. You need to follow it minute by minute, as people react to what's being said or done. Start your observations from the moment you meet and greet people, whether you're meeting them for the first time or they're your best friend you see every day.

WHAT TO OBSERVE IN A GREETING

Eyes

'The eye is the mirror of the soul.'

Yiddish proverb

Generally speaking the first thing you do when you greet someone is look each other up and down. As you're doing that, you take in lots of information about them, including their height, build, walk, posture, face, hair, make-up, clothing and accessories, and all manner of other things. You do all this in a fraction of a second, usually ending up looking at the face and making eye contact with the other person.

The amount of eye contact varies significantly between 50 and 90%, depending on your culture. Scandinavians will look you in the eyes much more than say, a Chinese or Japanese person would. In some cultures it's considered disrespectful to look someone in the eyes, while in others it is a sign of respect.

Taking cultural differences out of the equation, you won't always get full eye contact anyway. Sometimes you won't get any at all. Shy, nervous and less confident people won't give you much, whereas confident people will happily engage you eye to eye. There's a sign to look out for right from the off.

In the initial seconds of a greeting you'll see the other person's eyebrows move up and down momentarily. It's known as an 'eyebrow flash'. If you've never noticed it before you will now, even though it lasts less than a quarter of second in most cases. It's a non-verbal 'hello'. In itself, a sign of acknowledgement and/or interest.

If you were stood with a friend on one side of the road holding a conversation, and another friend walked along the other side of the street, you might just give them an eyebrow flash. No words needed, you've acknowledged them and said 'Hello, my friend'.

Look for this eyebrow flash when you greet people. It's a reasonably good indicator of how they feel about meeting you right there, right then. If you don't get it, then maybe they don't want to be meeting you, or they have something else on their mind.

If you don't see it, it's not the greatest start to a meeting.

Smiles

Eye contact is only one element of the greeting. We also tend to smile, but not all smiles express happiness. We smile in sad circumstances too. Ever been to a funeral and just looked at someone with that knowing smile?

There are lots of different smiles. Some are very genuine expressions of happiness, joy and love, while others can denote a sarcastic know-it-all attitude. Not all smiles are good!

Most of us smile when we greet people so it's worth taking notice of what the smile is saying when you get it.

How many smiles do you think you have?

This is a tricky one because it depends on what studies you look at, but I reckon there are at least 12 distinct smiles. The others are just slight variations.

Cute

Sarcastic

Embarrassed

Grimace

Contented

Joyous

Pride

Alluring

Cheeky

Confident

Coy

Excitement

Working together

The eyes, eyebrow flash and smile all work together. Certain muscles simply won't work properly if the smile is forced or fake. The orbicularis oculi muscle runs around the eye socket and is fired when we smile, causing the cheek under the bottom lid to scrunch up and the corners of the eyes to wrinkle. This works in harmony with zygomatic muscles that are at the corners of the mouth pulling up towards the corner of the eyes.

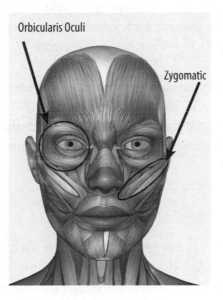

This forms wrinkle lines often referred to as crow's-feet or laughter lines. There's a difference between the two. Crow's-feet are quite straight lines coming out from the corners of the eyes, whereas laughter lines have a kink, so the line runs under the eyelid, which is squeezed by the orbicularis oculi and comes to a point at the outside corner of the eye, or just below, and then the lines straighten out.

Take a look at the two pictures opposite and you'll be able to see the difference. It's a tiny one but that's what you are learning here. Being aware of the subtle changes in muscle tone and what they mean helps you decode it all.

EXERCISE

Smile at yourself whilst looking in a mirror – even if you don't have too many lines they should show up. Now look closely at the outside edges of your eyes – do your facial creases have a slight upward kink just below the corner of your eyelid or do the lines go straight back from it?

If you have an upward kink chances are you spend a lot of time smiling and laughing. However, in my experience, if your lines go straight back then you're probably a little more reserved and may not show your expressions as readily as others.

There's an old saying from Abraham Lincoln: 'By forty you have the face you deserve'. In most cases that's very true because we pull the same facial expressions day in, day out. The lines created in the skin by our facial muscles pulling tight with each of our expressions get deeper and longer the more we use them. If you frown a lot, you get lines in your forehead just above your nose.

If you laugh a lot you'll get laughter lines round your eyes, mouth and cheeks.

Funnily enough, just searching for the right smile pictures to use here, has actually brought a smile to my own face. That's the thing about smiles. If they're genuine, you just warm to them. They make you want to smile right back. Just looking at another person smiling is contagious. Well, unless it's a demented one.

Here's a little poem I came across many years ago. It just about sums up everything in a smile.

A smile costs nothing but gives much.

It enriches those who receive without making poorer those who give.

It takes but a moment, but the memory of it sometimes lasts forever.

None is so rich or mighty that he can get along without it and none is so poor that he cannot be made rich by it.

Yet a smile cannot be bought, begged, borrowed, or stolen, for it is something that is of no value to anyone until it is given away.

Some people are too tired to give you a smile.

Give them one of yours, as none needs a smile, so much as he who has no more to give.

Author unknown

Whatever the expression, the more you use it, the more it becomes etched on your face with age. It's not an absolute rule but, more often than not, a person's natural facial lines are a good indicator of their natural emotional state and their general disposition in life, whether it's happy, grumpy, sad, etc.

FIRST IMPRESSIONS LAST LONGEST

When you're meeting someone for the first time you'll take in information about their appearance at an unconscious level – we do it all the time without even realizing. What I want to do with this book is help you actively look at someone's facial lines and see what they tell you.

Take a look at the faces of your friends, family and co-workers. Do the lines in their faces correspond to their nature?

In tests, young children were shown numerous photographs of other children and asked to rate them as nice or naughty. Almost every child in the tests rated the pictures the same, and they were right. The children rated nice were friendly and outgoing, whereas the children rated naughty were indeed the more adventurous and mischievous.

We seem to have an innate ability to decode the face and facial expressions of others right from an early age and we do it, for the most part, without conscious interference. We just get a hunch, a gut feeling.

UNIVERSAL FACIAL EXPRESSIONS

There's been a lot of work done in the area of universal facial expressions, and there do seem to be a certain number of facial expressions that are recognized around the world, by just about every person on the planet.

They are:

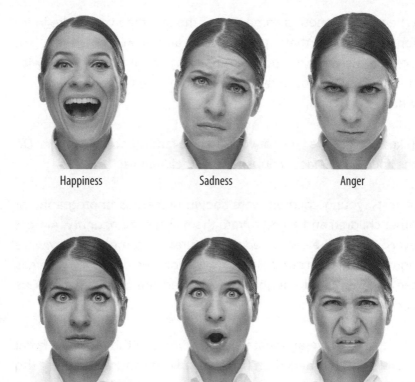

Happiness	Sadness	Anger

Fear	Surprise	Disgust

Micro expressions

During a greeting it's quite common to see one of these universal expressions, giving you information about how someone feels immediately. Sometimes you will see one of these expressions but only momentarily, before it's gone in a flash, to be replaced by the expression the person *thinks* you want to see.

Let's say you bump into an old friend or work colleague you haven't seen for years, and let's just say they owe you money. As your eyes meet and they recognize it's you, it dawns on them that they still haven't paid you back. You might see the fear expression flash across their face, to be replaced in a split second by a smile, as they pretend they're pleased to see you.

Another time you'll see it, but in reverse. You've probably done this yourself. You see someone bangs their elbow or stubs their toe, any sort of silly accident. Your face will start to crack a smile but immediately replace it with a sad face to show empathy with the injured party. Basically, you thought it was quite funny but don't want to show them that.

These tiny fleeting facial signals are known as micro expressions. They last less than half a second, but you can still pick them up quite easily just by looking at people's faces.

Micro expressions are incredibly useful for the simple fact that they are unconscious and show concealed emotion. They appear because the person displaying them hasn't had time to *think* about their response. They haven't had a chance to try to stop it before it's happened. For this reason they are 100% reliable.

If you see fear, then they are fearful. If you see happy they are happy. They may be fleeting, but don't ignore them. There is no mistaking what emotion the person just felt. They flashed it across their face for you to see.

MACRO EXPRESSIONS

There's also another set of signals called macro expressions. These too flash across the face but last just slightly longer, between half a second and five seconds, according to research by Dr David Matsumoto of the training and research company Humintell, California. Macro expressions go on during normal interactions when there is no need to hide the emotion being felt. It's also one of the ways in which we show empathy and bond with the person speaking by acknowledging what they are saying with our facial expressions.

Posture

Posture is one of the things you tend to notice during a greeting. How you carry yourself says a lot about how the world perceives you. Do you walk with your head up, alert, meeting the world head on so to speak, or do you drop your head down, looking at the floor or out of the tops of your eyes?

When you're confident, there is a relaxed fluidity in your movements because there's no tension in your body. Conversely when you get tense, various muscles contract so your movements can become more rigid – even chicken-like in some cases.

Before you meet someone, it's always best if you can observe them without them knowing. Try looking out of a window or sitting outside a restaurant or coffee shop so that you can watch them approach or as they prepare to meet you. This way you get to see if there's a change in their posture. Do they go from being a bag of nerves, fumbling with folders, checking pockets and taking big deep breathes outside your meeting, before transforming into super-confident the minute they walk through the door?

A few years back I did some PR work with the British Chiropractic Association, and as part of their campaign they did some research, asking interviewers how they reacted to lazy posture. A full 60% said they wouldn't employ someone with bad posture. Similarly, 61% of people equate good posture to a confident personality.

You can see how someone is feeling just through their posture. You don't even have to be face-to-face with them. Next time you have the opportunity, find yourself somewhere to sit or stand, and just watch people passing by. Look at their body posture. If they're talking, that's even better as you'll see how their posture changes throughout an interaction. Leaning in towards the person they're talking to could indicate that they're showing interest. On the other hand, it could just as easily represent a threat, in which case you'd spot the other person pull their whole body away showing surprise or anger on their face.

Postural movements, such as leaning in, out and side to side, are quite big and very obvious. Start consciously noticing posture when you interact and you'll give yourself a choice about whether to change the conversation in response to a negative posture, or continue in the same vein if it's positive.

Positive posture is open and relaxed. People lean in toward anything they want to see, hear, smell, taste and touch more of. Negative posture on the other hand is closed and distant. People pull away from anything they don't like.

HEAD

Sitting on top of your shoulders and neck is a head, which you tilt and angle in association with the rest of your body, your facial expressions and your hand movements. If you see something like a cute baby or lambs in a field, you'll tilt your head to one side and say, 'Ahhh, that's so sweet'. As a general rule, head tilts to the side are a good sign, as is the head flicking slightly upward at about the same time as they give you an eyebrow flash. The two go together naturally and they're what you will see most of the time when meeting people.

The one to watch for in business greetings, particularly in a first meeting, is the head tilting slightly downward without the eyebrow flash. It's fine if it's a nod, that's a nod of approval or acknowledgement, but when the person you're greeting *keeps* their head angled down, that suggests you're dealing with someone who wants to be in control, a dominator. This person will want it all on their terms. You have been warned.

SO FAR SO GOOD

Remember what we've covered so far: eyes, eyebrows, smiles, micro expressions, posture and head angles – and we're still only at the greeting stage. It doesn't stop there though. Everything you've learned so far is also relevant further down the line as your greetings turn into meetings, negotiations and presentations.

The one bit I haven't covered so far in this section is what happens when we say 'hello'. We generally give and receive a handshake, hug, kiss or bow – maybe all of them, depending on our culture. The most common by far in business is the handshake, so here's a breakdown of what's happening when you make this everyday greeting. I think it will surprise you.

HANDSHAKE, HUG, KISS OR BOW

Handshakes

Shaking hands is one of few times people are actually allowed to touch each other in the workplace! Handshakes are pretty amazing things really, they're almost completely automatic. Walk round your workplace and stick your hand out to just about anyone and eight out of ten people will automatically shake your hand back without batting an eyelid – it's the natural thing to do.

I have tried this experiment many times with complete strangers and I thoroughly recommend you do the same. Walk up to someone you've never met before in your local high street, in a bar or restaurant to ask for directions, order drinks or whatever, and as you walk toward them, put your hand out in the normal handshaking way. Try it and you'll see just how automatic it is for complete strangers to happily shake your hand. When you think about it, this is a very strange phenomenon. Your body just goes onto autopilot. Like most of our body language, it's a habit. You stick your hand out, grab theirs, you both go shaky shaky a few times, say 'hello', then let go.

This simple automatic act has lots and lots of sensory feedback so I'll try to break it down as much as I can. There's hand angle, type of grip, amount of pressure, number of shakes, whether the arm goes up and down or just the hand.

There are basically four types of handshake (plus one very special one!):

- palm up

- palm down

- palms vertical

- double handed

- … and the José Mourinho or Special One.

Before you read on, it's worth noting that handshaking actually has a release moment where, if the hands have met fully, the finger tips start the process by letting go of the side of the other person's palm. If you pay attention, you can feel when this happens and know if it was you or them who released the handshake first. This is quite a useful mental note to take, as this is right at the beginning of your meeting and gives you another little insight, like the smile, the eye contact, eyebrow flash and all the other things you are putting together, into what sort of person this is and how best to handle them.

Palm up: the wet lettuce or dead fish

This handshake is normally very weak in pressure. You don't get full palm-to-palm contact, sometimes just the fingertips. Very few people like receiving a limp handshake, especially in the business world. It's like they're trying to take their hand away before you've had a chance to feel it.

People naturally associate, rightly or wrongly, that weak handshakes signify a weak personality. In my experience this is not true but it is perpetuated in many books and training courses on body language in the sales and marketing industry, which likes to stereotype and put people in boxes.

In fact, a weak, palm-up handshake is quite often given by people who have absolutely no reason to try and impose themselves on others. Either they've already made it in their industry or they are just very comfortable with themselves.

I've shaken the hands of millionaires and a few billionaires too. Some of them have had the most gentle, soft grip, palm up handshakes you're ever likely to receive. It's not always a sign of weakness. It can be a sign of power.

Palm down: the bone crusher or boss

This handshake is the complete opposite of palm up. It's usually firm or very firm in grip pressure. In business it's quite normal and often associated with dominance, control, and strength of character.

I've noticed that you usually get a tiny bit of warning when someone is about to give you a palm-down handshake. Their arm moves out very slightly from the body and comes around in sweeping movement. It has to do this to change the angle of the hand.

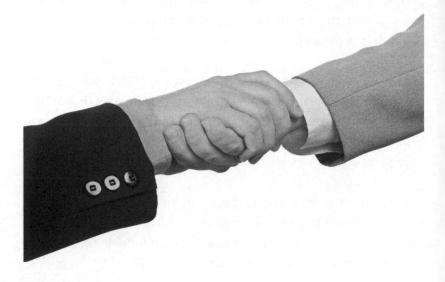

You'll have had your fair share of palm-down handshakes in your time. On the whole it's the more dominant, strong characters who give them. Maybe you use this type of handshake yourself? If you do, just be aware that it can be, and often is, perceived as too dominant and too controlling. It suggests you want to be the boss, especially if the grip pressure is too much and you hold on to the hand longer than you should. Remember the release moment mentioned above?

Palms vertical: the equalizer

This is the most common and preferred handshake in business, and life in general, as neither party is palm up or down. It's an equality handshake. That's not to say it's always equal though, as quite often one party will use excessive grip pressure to show a sign of dominance.

In this handshake, the hand and arm move straight forward from the side of the body to meet the other person's, the hand doesn't turn at all.

The double hander: the controller or bonding

The double hander is exactly what it says; where someone shakes using both hands. The right hand grips the other person's right hand and the left hand is used to clasp over the top of their right hand. Sometimes the left hand grip will extend further up the arm.

The higher up the arm the grip from the left is, the more control that person is generally trying to exert.

However, it's not always a controlling gesture. The double hander can also be a sign of bonding and empathy. You'll often see this in social situations, certainly more so than in business, unless the relationship between the two people is already well established as a good one.

Imagine you were meeting someone for the first time and you'd never spoken to them before. The person walks up and gives you a double hander with their left hand high up round your right bicep and tricep. How does it make you feel about them?

Now, imagine the same scenario but this time you're meeting your best friend at a coffee shop. Now how does it feel? Totally different I'll bet. You see it's quite alright to use the left hand when you know someone and you have some sort of relationship with them. Where it's appropriate it feels comfortable and not at all out of place.

In business it's not the norm. If you do ever get a handshake like this, make a mental note of it. I am always quite wary of people who give me double-handed shakes without knowing me. If it happens, always remember to look at the face, as the eye contact and smile should tell you whether it's one of warmth and bonding or a controlling, dominance clue.

Another thing to take note of is whether the arm is bent at the elbow or straight. You'll have heard the expression 'keeping someone at arm's length' before. It's another one of those common phrases that relates to how we use our body to keep people away. An arm's length is about the closest you want anyone who may present any sort of threat to you.

If you measured the distance between the bodies of two people shaking hands, you'd find that the average distance between them is about the same length as the arm itself, 60–80cms from the tip of the fingers to the start of the shoulder. One theory on the 'arm's length' distance is that it's an instinctive personal safety measure. After all, it's not easy to hit someone unless you're within an arm's length.

A straightened arm, locked at the elbow, isn't very flexible and, in my experience, neither are the people who give them. By the same token you don't want a floppy arm that you can shake all over the place. A handshake without any strength can show that the person is easily swayed.

The José Mourhino

That's not it's real name but it is the special one among handshakes. It's known only to a handful of people on this planet and I'm about to share it with you. What you do with this is entirely up to you, but I hope you will only use it for good.

It's actually known as a 'handshake interrupt'. It's a very strange phenomenon that comes out of the world of hypnosis and NLP.

Remember earlier when I was talking about habits and patterns of behaviour being all but 100% automatic? Well, as we've seen, handshakes also fall into this category. They're completely automatic, so if you interrupt a handshake in the middle, the brain momentarily goes 'What happened?' At that point the mind is confused because handshakes don't normally get interrupted in the middle. It's normally grip, shake, let go.

There are lots of different ways to interrupt a handshake and lots of different ways to use the effect it has on the brain. Derren Brown has used the technique in several of his TV shows and live performances over the last ten years or so. He's very good at doing it in different ways.

If you wanted to put someone into an hypnotic trance you could. I'm not going to explain how but a quick Google of 'handshake interrupt' will take you to literally hundreds of videos of hypnotists from around the world showing exactly how to do it. All I would say is treat this with caution and if you want to try it, do it on close friends and family but ask permission first – although you shouldn't explain exactly what it is or the surprise interrupt will be gone.

Interruption actually works with lots of automatic patterns. Can you think of any other automatic actions which could be interrupted?

The hug

Hugging isn't normal business practice in the US or the UK, but it's commonplace across Europe, Latin America, Russia and some parts of the Middle East where it is often accompanied by a kiss or kisses, depending on where you are.

Incidentally, it's not uncommon for a Saudi businessman in his own country to handshake, hug and then walk hand in hand with a new found business colleague. This is, of course, assuming it is a man. This can be most disconcerting to the average British or American businessman. It's not that common for businessmen to walk hand in hand down the road or through an airport terminal.

Hugs, though, are generally good things and make us feel nice if they're being given by someone we like. Not so nice if you don't like the person you're with.

As with all body language, there are subtle differences in the way people hug. For example, you can just use the top half of your body to lean forward – think celebrities air kissing – or you can move the whole body so it's almost belly to belly, which is much more intimate. We don't generally allow people to get that close unless we have a bond with them! It's a territory and space thing, which we'll cover in more depth later.

The essential part to note in any hug is how close it is. If it's close, does it feel comfortable coming from this person? Have they got good reason to hug you like this? Have you met before? Is it just a cultural thing? Do your research before you go to any foreign country, especially if you are doing business.

Kisses

Kisses are a minefield.

This is always an awkward one; you go to shake hands they come in for the kiss, you respond hesitantly with one kiss, they go for a second and a third, maybe a fourth and even fifth.

What if you are the initiator – which cheek do you start with? Actually, most people go for the right cheek first.

Kissing greetings in business are rare in the UK and really only happen on a regular basis in industries like fashion, beauty and the media. For the average city banker it's not the done thing.

Like hugs, kisses are generally meant as a sign of friendship, love and affection, but as with smiles and the celebrity air kiss, they aren't always real. They're only meant to look real.

The best advice I can give here is to be led by the kisser. That's to say, if you're not into kissing and you meet someone in a business situation that goes for it, unless you have a real aversion, just go with their lead. If they go for one just respond with one, if it's two go two yourself. That way you can't really get it wrong.

Like the handshake you have a choice either to be the initiator or the responder. Obviously I recommend wholeheartedly that you play with kisses and be the initiator, as long as it's appropriate in your industry, and just gauge the reactions for yourself. Kisses can be a great bonder and a nice way to start and finish a meeting.

A couple of years back I heard of a very strange phenomenon going round London – of business execs kissing on the lips as a sign of trust. When I heard about this I spoke to another expert in the field, Judi James, who'd also heard about it although neither of us actually knew anyone who had experienced it.

Can you imagine that? You meet someone for the first time, have a meeting, do a business deal then kiss on the lips. I don't think so! If you are one of those rare people who experienced this, please get in contact with me, I'd love to hear of the circumstances and reactions.

Bowing

You will very rarely come across bowing outside Asia but you do still see it occasionally in business meetings when dealing with representatives or companies from Asian countries.

The simple act of bowing is a sign of respect in those cultures and the lower the bow, the higher the status of the person receiving it. Not only is it a sign of respect but one of agreement, a yes. After all, what is the movement we use to signify a yes? It's a quick single nod or an up and down movement of the head; it's a shortened bow.

In some cultures people bow the head slightly with the hands pressed together palm to palm in front of the body, their fingers pointing skyward – this is known as the 'namaste' and is often accompanied by the word itself, 'namaste'. It's very common greeting across India.

Bowing is courteous and quite formal so if you encounter it don't bow back unless you feel comfortable doing so. If you bow, be sure you know your place in the hierarchy or you won't get it right and may offend, when your intention was to ingratiate yourself. It's someone else's culture, not yours, and unlike the kiss, which is fairly easy to follow and get right, the bow is not. If your normal greeting is a handshake, the best advice is to stick with what you know.

SUMMARY

That's it, on what you probably thought was a simple greeting. You'll now realize just how much there is going on in those first few seconds.

All the body language you see in a greeting you'll see at other points. Sometimes it'll have the same meaning but other times it'll be completely different – it is the situations and circumstances that will determine the meaning not the movements on their own.

Here are a few things to try for yourself based on what we've looked at in this chapter.

- Smile. Don't. Instead of smiling, just use an eyebrow flash with an upward flick of the head. What reaction do you get?

- Eye contact. Try giving people more or less than is normal for you (you might find it hard to give extended eye contact if you're naturally quite shy). How do people respond to this? How does it make you feel?

- Head tilt. Walk towards people you're about to greet with your head tilted slightly to one side or tilt it up or down.

- Handshake. Change it. Play around with palm up weak, palm down firm or even double handed. Hold the grip longer or less than normal. Get your hand out first or let them lead.

- Hug, kiss or bow. Add one or all of them to your greetings.

Don't try all these things at once and only try what you feel comfortable with. You've got to be pretty playful and be fully prepared to get some strange reactions!

5

MEETINGS

After the greeting comes the meeting. Unlike social encounters, which are just for the enjoyment of seeing friends and family, business meetings always have a purpose, or at least they should.

Meetings come in various shapes and sizes, from standing in a coffee shop to the boardroom of a smart office complex and everything in between. Generally speaking, the purpose of any meeting is to impart or gather information, discuss it and hopefully come to some form of agreement.

Meetings should have a start, a middle and an end, and over the period of time the meeting takes, points being discussed or information imparted will ebb and flow with positives, negatives and ambivalence.

Your job is to observe the body movements, signals and gestures right from the start, and to continue to monitor them throughout. This will help you understand the people you're meeting better.

THE CHRONOLOGY OF A MEETING

Before most meetings get going there is a bit of social chit chat. You talk about the weather or the journey to the office, for example.

SOFT AND HARD MEETINGS

Soft meetings cover normal day-to-day interactions such as team briefings, updates or quick requests for information, where there's no real pressure or influence being put on anyone.

Hard meetings are less common. These are for disciplining staff, negotiating contracts, dressing down a supplier and so on. If it's you running the meeting then you might actually want to influence the situation by using what's at your disposal within the environment.

However, always remember that if you are not in control of the meeting and it's at someone else's premises, you need to be observant and pick up on how they may have deliberately set out their territory.

This is a good time to observe. Most people are more relaxed talking pleasantries than they are talking about the purpose of the meeting. When you get into the meeting itself, the atmosphere changes, not always, but most of the time, even if it's a subtle shift.

Observing people when they're relaxed gives you some form of baseline behaviour. As the meeting progresses you can spot the shifts in attitudes, emotions and feelings as you talk over the subject. What you talk about and the results achieved can be greatly influenced by the environment itself. This is particularly true when sitting round a table, which is where we conduct most meetings, so let's start there.

Tables

Meeting rooms have tables in just about every shape you can think of, and each has advantages and disadvantages. The bottom line is, tables either have angles or they don't. If it's your office and you have a choice over furniture, go for round or oval for more condu-cive meetings. Rectangular and square tables are the most com-mon, but their sides create angles and your position or angle to the person or people you're meeting can dramatically influence how well you get on with them.

The trouble with most tables is that we also tend to create imagi-nary middles to them, your half, my half. If you sit opposite each other, even on a round or oval table, you'll split it. Look at these pictures and you'll see what I'm talking about.

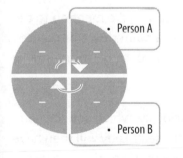

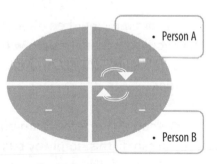

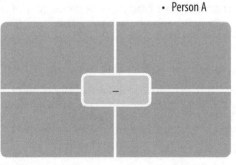

If you plan it out, you can use a table with angles for harder meetings and without for soft. That's the ideal scenario. One of the best ways to cover both soft and hard meetings in the same office is to have your main desk as a standard rectangle or square, and a second smaller low round table in the corner for more friendly informal chats.

Where to sit

Depending on the whether the meeting you're having is a hard or soft one, you have a choice. If it's a softer meeting then you can let the other person choose where to sit. This will give them an added sense of comfort and you can adapt your position relative to them. Alternatively, you can direct them with an open palm gesture, using an eyebrow flash in the process.

If it's a hard meeting then direct the person you're meeting to the chair you want them to sit in with either a palm down or pointed finger movement. This is more forceful and controlling, more like an order.

An alternative is to force them unconsciously, which sounds hard, but you can do this simply by taking your seat. They will then have no choice but to sit more or less where you want them to, especially when you angle your body in the direction of the chair where you want them to sit.

Another technique is to stand with your hand on the back of a chair and just wait for them to sit. Generally it will be assumed that you are going to sit in that chair and they will sit opposite. If you really want to make things awkward, once the other person has sat down, sit in the chair *next* to the one you have your hand on. This creates an odd angle between you and them, making things less comfortable for them. Very few people will shift up a chair to be equal again.

If you want to be truly horrible just remain standing, using the chair back as a great big barrier. Not only do you have the chair, but you also have the desk between you. You could even remain standing and walk around.

Again, knowing these things gives you choices. Here's how I personally used the seating to maximize my meeting with Capstone, publisher of this book.

I met my contact, Iain, at the reception of their offices in Chichester and we did the standard business grip and grin bit, then off to the meeting room with him directing the way, chatting, opening doors, etc. We entered the room, not his own office, but a room specifically designed for meetings of all sorts. You know the type – they're generally similar and quite sterile wherever you are, with plasma screens, big table, uniform chairs, etc. Iain then went off to get another colleague, Megan, who was to join us.

I spent this short time looking around the meeting room, standing by the big window looking out. I deliberately remained standing, as sitting would have meant I had no chance to change my position in relation to theirs. I'd be relying on them choosing a conducive position in relation to me.

We went through the meeting to a very satisfactory conclusion on all sides and when we were chatting I explained how I'd done specific things throughout our meeting to maximize it. After all, I only had one shot at this. One of the elements I explained was deliberately not sitting down before they were both back in the room. As soon as I mentioned it they cast their minds back to the beginning

A NOTE ON NOTES

Regardless of what your meeting is about, taking notes is commonplace. However, one simple mistake a lot of people make is that they ask questions then immediately look away to start writing, which just makes reading body language impossible. If you've got your head down taking notes, you're missing it all.

The best tactic is to switch it round the other way. Make your notes on what the person just said as you ask your next question, then look up and observe while they talk. This simple approach can completely change how much body language you observe. You'll probably take in close to 50% more.

of the meeting and it all made sense to them how these things can positively influence the outcome.

Chairs

I mentioned using a chair as a barrier above, but there are other ways to use chairs to send non-verbal messages.

Chairs, like desks and tables come in all sorts of weird and wonderful shapes and sizes. I've sat on what I call school chairs: little, horrible, metal-legged, plastic-backed things. I've sat in beautiful high-backed leather chairs with padded arm and head rests. I've even sat on the floor and on bean bags!

If you're meeting someone running their own company, they will normally have complete freedom over their office furniture, and will have chosen the chairs. What they've chosen will tell you something about their character. Look at their chair and then look at yours. What's the difference? Is theirs a nice, comfy, high-backed leather with all the bells and whistles, swivelling and rocking in all directions? Is yours the same or is it a lower grade chair?

One of the things about a swivel chair that can be used for power over a static one is that, in a swivel, the person sitting in it can angle their body and look away from you, all nonchalant, relaxed and in control. Second, it also offers them a desk/table to lean on, which can be used as another barrier. You can't do either.

But that's OK. If you've been reading up to now then you'll know that these subtle shifts can be clues to add to your observations, helping you decode who you are dealing with, what they think about, and what you are both saying, hearing, seeing, touching, tasting or smelling.

Chairs with arm rests can be useful. If you want to appear more confident. Sit with your elbows on them and your hands resting in your lap, or with just one elbow on a rest and the other hand/arm in your lap. This makes you bigger and gives you freedom to use your hands and arms as you speak.

Alternatively, if you want to come across as a little submissive, sit with your elbows inside the arm rests. It'll make you look smaller and more vulnerable. It'll also restrict your hand and arm movements a little as you'll have to lift them above the arm rest to use them fully.

If you want to appear a little cold or aloof, sit with your elbows poking out over the arm rests with your hands clasped across the front of your body or steepled for added superiority!

When seated behind a desk or table it is often difficult to see what the legs and feet are doing, but the signals they give off can be revealing.

You're not going to gain supernatural powers from reading this book that will enable you to see through tables and desks, but by watching the top half of the other person's body very carefully, you can see when they're jiggling their feet because their clothes or torso and shoulders will move at the same time as their legs. Often when people do this it's a sign of frustration, boredom, pressure or nerves, it's like they want to physically use their feet to get away. They might also want the toilet!

EXERCISE

Sit behind a table/desk with a large mirror in front of you and look at your body while your feet and legs remain still. Then start jiggling your foot/feet around and you'll see exactly what I mean and how visible it can be. Try jiggling your foot/ feet at different speeds and in different seated positions. Notice how it changes.

Stand up meetings

The other most common type of meeting is stood up in the middle of an office, on the factory floor, in a coffee shop or bar, etc. There may still be a table involved, but no chairs. When there are no chairs, people will often lean on walls, table tops or whatever they can.

Standing meetings are better in a lot of ways. They tend to be quicker by virtue of the fact that most people don't like standing around and, without tables, no one has anything to support them. Standing up also reveals more of the body.

Stand-up meetings, by virtue of the fact that there is nothing hiding the body, can make people feel uncomfortable. You'll often see them use some form of barrier; crossing arms is very common, so is using folders. If you see someone walking through your office with a folder in their hand, stop them to ask a question and watch the folder come up in front of them like a shield. That's exactly what barriers are, mini shields to protect us from possible attack, either verbal or physical.

HOW BODY LANGUAGE DEVELOPS OVER THE COURSE OF A MEETING

People don't just sit still in meetings, they shift their body position, their head angle, their arms and hands will beat in time with their words like a conductor with a baton. Their feet and legs will cross, uncross, move around. Their facial expressions will change moment to moment along with all manner of other things. Your goal is to master this ebb and flow: observe it, decode it and adapt to it.

The more body language you can observe, the more clued up you'll be when it comes to making decisions about whether you do business with AN Other Company Ltd, or employ a particular interviewee. You're already doing all of this unconsciously. All I'm getting you to do is to observe more of what's on display all the time so that you can make *better* decisions and have more choices.

HAND AND ARM MOVEMENTS

Palms

We covered hands in Greetings (Chapter 4) when talking about handshakes and some of what you learned there still applies in certain situations, particularly the palm-up and palm-down gestures.

Think for a moment about all the people you know both personally and professionally. Ask yourself, do they talk mainly with their palms angled down with stiff hand and arm movements or do they go for palms up with the hands rolling loosely on wrists?

Then ask yourself how you perceive each of them? Do you perceive them as bossy, moaning, someone who likes to get their own way or a pushover?

Chances are the person who uses more palm-down hand movements comes across as the bossy one, a moaner or someone who likes to get their own way. People who use more upturned movements during conversations, with their palms visible, come across as open, friendly and non-threatening.

You may never have noticed how other people – or you for that matter – use your own hands. You just know they wave around a lot. Well the time has come for you to start taking notice and observing what's right in front of you.

You can deliberately use palm down gestures to appear confident and assertive, or go the other way and give the impression of being passive and submissive by using palm up and open movements.

During your usual Monday morning planning meeting you decide you want a certain member of staff to go to another office to pick up some files. You can use the same words and same tone of voice, but your gestures will completely change the sense:

> 'John, can you go to over to our other office and collect last year's files on absenteeism, please, they'll be waiting at reception for you.'

Using palm-up, open and visible hand signals to accompany the words will make it appear like they're doing you a favour, helping you out. By turning your hand so that the palm is facing slightly downward, the words become much more assertive. In fact, it becomes more like an order. Try it for yourself and see.

Of course, if you want to be really direct and forthright you could point a finger at John and in the direction of the other office, but this would be a little extreme.

I mentioned these palm up, palm down and pointed finger gestures earlier when discussing the various ways to direct people to chairs in meetings. It really works effectively and lets people know you're not messing around. If you understand the gestures and use them in communication yourself, it will help other people understand when you're emphasizing something, being serious or taking control.

For example, if you call a member of staff in for a meeting to discipline them over a recent bout of absences, but showing your palms as you do it, chances are they won't take your threats of further action seriously. On the other hand, if your palms are down and you use downward movements as you point out the possible consequences of further absence, your words will carry much more weight. Now they have silent power behind them.

If you want to see this for yourself, then get the mirror out again and just stand or sit in front of it. Choose whatever words you like, just say them the same each time with the same tone of voice, only adjust your hands from palm up to palm down and try it with the finger pointing too. You'll see how completely different it comes across. It's only a small thing but it has a major impact on your audience and is an effective way to use your hands to soften or harden your message.

Precision grip and incomplete grip

The hands are crucial and are used to convey all sorts of messages, from strong emphatic gestures that add weight and power to what you're saying, right the way through to the tiny, incomplete movements that reveal that you are not as certain about something as your words suggest. The precision grip and the incomplete grip are two great examples.

Precision grip is where the finger and thumb come together to form a complete circle. You'll see this often when people are talking about a crucial point that they feel you or their audience must understand. It's a favourite of just about every politician on the planet, usually accompanied by words like 'We have thoroughly costed out every single pound of this budget and I commend it to the House'.

Business people use it when they want their audience, whether that's one or many, to understand that they have whatever they're talking about under control.

The incomplete grip is the flip side to the precision grip, where the index finger and thumb don't quite meet. They nearly do but just stop short. This is used often as well. Used consciously, it is a visual way of expressing that something isn't quite finished yet, isn't completely under control. In this case, it matches the words exactly: 'Yes we've got the widgets into manufacture but we're not quite there on overall label design'. The finger and thumb are not quite there in completing the gesture either.

Something else to look out for though is where someone says they have everything under control and running to plan but use the incomplete grip at the same time. The gesture would indicate otherwise. It suggests they're a bit vague or there's a gap in their thinking. This should set the alarm bells ringing. If you notice this action accompanying confident sounding words, you might want to probe a little deeper.

Wrists, hands and fingers

Another element I mentioned briefly earlier was the wrists in relation to the hands and whether they're loose and relaxed or stiff and rigid. Loose and relaxed usually corresponds very nicely to conducive meetings where people are being open and exchanging views. No one is controlling, no one is being forceful. They're usually palm up and visible as well.

Stiff wrist movements, like the palm down, show emphasis, power, seriousness. There is a whole host of hand signals that go with the rigid locked hand and arm moving as one. We'll call them cutting/chopping, sweep, fists and fingers.

1. *Cutting/chopping*. Cutting and chopping actions symbolically cut through or separate issues being discussed. You'll see these movements often in meetings with stiff wrists. Watch any of the three main political leaders at the Dispatch Box in the House of Commons and you see plenty of examples. The speakers push forward with the hand and arm moving as one or pull it back towards themselves or use a sweeping action out to the side.

2. *Sweep*. The sweeping action symbolizes sweeping issues to the side or up and away. It can be made with loose or stiff wrists. Done with a loose wrist, it's more of a flick. It shows that the issue is a small one, a minor irritation or an inconvenience. If you see the sweep done with stiff wrists, you know it's more important.

3. *Fists*. When someone gets frustrated, annoyed or stressed, they will often go from using a pointed finger to curling the finger in to create a fist. Making a fist of course is a clear sign that you want to hit something or someone, and this is usually expressed physically by either pounding the fist on a desk, up in the air or pushing it forward like a punch.

    If someone is frustrated with themselves they will often bang their own body, particularly their heads, with their clenched fists.

    Fist gestures can be a positive signal too. For instance, when you've achieved something you might punch the air. You'll also see it as a small air punch when someone is happy too. It's like a thumbs-up, OK signal. Some people, usually men, do it several times very fast as though they were a boxer punching a bag.

4. *Fingers*. Fingers are used consciously to count, point, gesture and direct but, unconsciously, they can also show signs of frustration, excitement, anticipation and impatience.

Pointed finger

We use pointed fingers to give physical directions or to highlight something. We use them like a conductor uses a baton to beat in time with our words. We wag them back and forth to indicate a

'No'. We also use them to threaten when pushed toward another person.

Just as people who talk with lots of palm-down hand movements can come across as bossy and controlling, like they're always giving the orders, so too can those who talk with a pointed finger.

Interlocked

Sitting with interlocked fingers forms a barrier. You sometime see them raised in front of the body, chin or face. The higher it is the more of a barrier it becomes.

Steeple

You'll also see the fingers not interlocked but with just the tips touching. This is known as 'steepling' simply because it's resembles a church steeple. In most cases this is a confidence or even superiority signal.

Interlocked steeple

This is simply a combination of the two with the index fingers steepling and the rest interlocked forming a very high barrier. The example below, with the head down being supported by the hands, shows high tension.

Interlocked fingers can become locked if you are in a stressful situation because you tend to squeeze them tight together. You can often see white knuckles appearing when this happens.

Hand supporting head

Hands supporting the head can mean anything from boredom and sadness to interest and desire. In this case, you have to look at the facial expressions too.

Hands behind head or neck

Sitting with your hands clasped at the back of your neck or head is another one of those poses you really don't want to be seeing or doing yourself in business. It's primarily a male pose that conveys confidence, superiority and arrogance. You see it a lot when someone is either talking up themselves or their company. If someone else is talking and the listener adopts this pose, it says, 'I know I'm right regardless of what you say'.

It can be a pose that people go into after stretching, but if it is you'll know the difference by the way it's done. They'll normally stretch the arms out or upward before entering this position. Generally the facial expression will change and you will see a physical stretching of the body.

Notice the crossing of the ankles. Like crossed arms they are often used as a defence or negative barrier.

Arm crossing

Let's get this one out of the way now because in my experience, nine out of ten people think it's a negative sign, but actually it doesn't have to be.

How do you sit when relaxing watching TV at home? Chances are it's either with your hands in your lap, maybe one hand on the arm rest or with your arms crossed comfortably over your tummy. If it's a position you adopt for comfort, clearly it's not negative. It can be a relaxed position too.

In business meetings and presentations it can often signal that the person speaking has finished talking. They cross their arms as a signal to you that it's your turn now.

There are also many different ways you can cross your arms – with relaxed hands, clenched fists, thumbs sticking up, gripping the biceps. They all have slightly differing meanings.

Do you even know how you instinctively cross your arms? I'm guessing not. Why would you?

EXERCISE

Go on – cross your arms now and see how you do it.

The most common arm cross is for your left arm to end up on top of your right arm. It doesn't mean anything if yours is the other way round as far as I'm aware, it's just the way people end up doing it. Once that's your habit, you stick with it forever, like everything else.

Assuming you've crossed your arms now, take a look at how your hands are positioned. Are they loose and relaxed with the left hand under the right arm just by the elbow and with the right hand resting in the crease of the left elbow? Your fingers might be round the bicep slightly. Some people grip their biceps tight. Look for excessive gripping of the arm; look at the knuckles to see if they are white.

Two other positions to look for are as above but with clenched fists, or sticking up thumbs. I call this second one the 'barrister' or 'headmaster'. It's where the fingers go under the armpits and the thumbs point upward, almost as though they are holding the lapels of a gown. Neither position is sending good signals but remember it might be someone's relaxed position, so look also at the shoulders.

Shoulders

Movements of the shoulders are almost always completely un-conscious. It's where lots of people feel tension and how many headaches start. Tightening all the muscles along the shoulder and neck creates a tension headache.

Shoulders raise up and inward when you feel tense or unsure. It's not uncommon to hear someone say 'Yes' but accompany it by raising and holding their shoulders or just giving a quick shrug up and down, showing their uncertainty. If this happens, you know they are actually caught between a yes and a no. It's exactly the same as when people say 'Yes' with their mouths but shake their head for 'No'.

It works the other way round too. But, in the case of shoulders going from raised to lowered, this shows tension being released or even giving up on something. Typically you'll see this whenever someone is put on the spot for an answer or they feel obliged to give the answer they think you want to hear.

When you see shoulder shrugs you have a choice to question further, adapt. Or just make a mental note. Either way, whatever it is you were just talking about isn't clear in their mind – or their answer was just plain false!

MIRRORING AND MATCHING

I mentioned mirroring briefly at the beginning of this book. I'll cover it in a little more depth now along with matching, which is essentially the same except the other way round.

In mirroring, you're basically copying someone's movements but in reverse. If they pick a drink up from the table with their right hand, you pick your drink up with your left hand, a mirrored reflection of their actions.

Matching is when you do exactly the same movement as theirs: they move their right hand, you move your right hand.

Matching is used a lot by therapists to gain an even deeper level of rapport with their clients. A downside is that it can cause the therapist to take on the problems of the client because they are so in rapport with them. Not good!

Mirroring/matching are interchangeable through any interaction. Sometimes two people will mirror, like picking a drink up with the opposite hand, other times they'll match and pick their drink up with the same hand.

It doesn't matter whether there's mirroring or matching, if it's happening it's generally a positive thing that naturally occurs when people are getting on. You don't have to force it, it just happens.

However, not all mirroring/matching is positive. It can be negative too.

When two people are arguing, they'll often stand toe to toe, leaning towards one another, jutting their chins forward, bearing their teeth and gesticulating wildly with their hands while they shout and scream. That's negative mirroring/matching.

In almost every body language book I've ever read, the author has stated that you should mirror someone to build rapport by copying their every move. Sorry, but you shouldn't. Why? Because if you just copy someone in an attempt to build rapport, most people will spot it very quickly, causing the complete opposite effect. We are naturally wary of people who copy us. When you spot it, you'll know it's being done deliberately to get you onside for whatever reason. That's a sure-fire way to create suspicion.

DIFFERENT TECHNIQUES FOR MIRRORING/ MATCHING

These are specific ways you can mirror and match that are pretty much undetectable. Again these techniques are used in hypnosis and NLP.

Posture

You can comfortably mirror or match the way someone sits or stands without causing alarm. Like I said, this happens naturally anyway. If they lean forward towards you when they're telling you something, you can lean in toward them to show your interest. It's your choice.

Breathing rate

This isn't as hard as you might think, just listen. Not to their actual breathing but to their speaking. If they are talking, they have to be breathing out. When they get to the end of their words they'll breathe again, so just do the same if you can.

Blinking rate

In hypnosis, both stage acts and therapists copy blinking and breathing rate as one of the ways of putting people into a trance. It's known as a non-verbal induction. First you copy their blinking rate, then change yours, keeping the eyes shut momentarily longer each time you blink, slowing down the breathing as well. Very soon they will be following your pattern and you can lead them into a trance state. There are many examples on YouTube (where else?). Just search 'non-verbal inductions'.

Now I'm not suggesting you hypnotize your business colleagues into a trance state but, by using the same techniques, which were developed to gain rapport with resistant clients in therapy, you can create strong connections without falling into the traps a lot of people do around mirroring or matching.

Speech pattern

Technically this bit shouldn't really be in a book on non-verbal communication, but by matching someone's speech rate you actually end up having to breathe at roughly the same rate as them anyway, which will also have the effect of putting you more in sync. That's the whole point of mirroring or matching: to put you on the same level.

Facial expressions

If someone is telling you a sad story, chances are they will display sad body signals such as drooped shoulders, head and facial expressions. If you're feeling empathetic towards their plight, then you will return their displays of emotion. You don't have to, of course: you can choose not to show any signs of empathy and very quickly most people will realize you are not interested.

Touch

Mirroring touch is not always a good idea in the business world, but it is a good way of bonding and it's another thing that happens naturally when people are getting on well.

You see it in the workplace when teams have worked together to achieve something. When they've pulled it off they'll shake hands, slap backs, hug and even kiss. Watch any team sport, any election victory or a space shuttle landing. You'll see these teams that have been working together to get to where they want and you'll see them doing exactly this sort of thing.

What have you got to lose?

Knowing how to mirror or match properly is an extremely useful tool to have in your belt for the simple fact that we don't always hit it off with people straight away. Being able to nudge it along a little is beneficial to both parties.

If you don't, what other options have you got? Stilted conversation with lots of awkward silences before you make your excuses and leave.

I suggest you play with mirroring and matching people. As with everything else you're learning, it's truly the only way to see what works for you. Unless you at least try some of these things you'll never know.

You may not feel 100% confident about trying out the techniques, but what do you have to lose? Who on earth is ever going to pick up that you are copying their breathing, blinking or speech pattern?

If you want to gain a bit of confidence in mirroring and matching before you try some of it for yourself, just watch people in any coffee shop, restaurant or bar. You can see how people sit and stand from quite a distance. To observe breathing, blinking and speech patterns you'll have to be reasonably close, a couple of tables away.

Take a look and find the people who immediately strike you as getting on well – laughing, smiling, nodding, maybe touching each other. Just note mentally or physically what movements and facial expressions they mirror or match.

After you're done with the happy people, look for those who aren't immediately giving off the same positive body language. Find a situation where people appear not to be getting on and you will see for yourself just how many things get mirrored back and forth, even if they're negative. Having read this far, you will pick up on what's happening, and you will know that you now have a little collection of techniques at your disposal for when you want to adapt a situation.

As I've mentioned, I'm a registered therapist in many different disciplines and some of the clients I see are not exactly happy to be there confronting issues they want to change. As a consequence, their body language is often quite closed; they won't make eye contact, preferring to stare into the middle ground or off into the distance, sitting with their arms and legs crossed tightly.

With clients like this, I have two options.

1.   I can do the complete opposite to them and show positive, open and friendly body language with lots of smiles and eye contact.

2.   I can mirror or match pretty much what they are doing.

It's down to me to choose the best route, based on the first few seconds after we've met, shaken hands and done the greeting bit.

Generally, I go with positive open body language initially, but if that gets me nowhere then I switch to match their confrontational or negative stance. Believe it not, I've found that showing most people the same disinterest they show me makes them think, 'Hey I came here for your help and now you're not doing what I expected'.

This often turns things around and they become the one who wants me to be interested in order to help them. Suddenly they start opening up and telling me all about their problems. Then we're getting somewhere.

If that doesn't work and they still don't engage with me, I employ a subtle influencing trick, gradually shifting from mirroring their negativity (crossed arms and legs, no smiles, very little eye contact) to more positive body language.

This is a very effective technique. First I uncross my arms and just rest them on my stomach or in my lap. Then I start using one hand to gesture outward from my body. Soon I introduce the other hand too, sometimes using one hand and other times both.

I might then uncross my legs and put one out straight in front of me with the other one bent at the knee in a relaxed position under it.

I've now gone from the crossed arms and legs closed off position, to gesturing with my hand movements out from my own body towards them, like an offering. My body language is saying 'I'll give you something if you give me something back'.

Having options is the key to getting on with the widest range of people possible. The more people you get on with, the more positive your outcomes.

Play with mirroring and matching. See what happens. It's a matter of how you present yourself in different situations. Let's face it – we are all presenting ourselves to the world every single day. You might as well make the best presentation you can.

SUMMARY

There are all sorts of different forms of meetings but essentially they are for exchanging information, which you can influence by simply making the most of what is available to you.

Meetings also take place in all sorts of environments; if it's yours, use it to your advantage by utilizing the furniture; if you can move things around, do it and see how you they can change the tone.

Whether it's your environment or not you can at least control the way you use your hands to add more impact to your verbal message.

Generally speaking, the most important thing to notice with any meeting is how much mirroring or matching there is, for the simple reason that it means you are both, or all, in sync with each other.

You'll find that in good meetings there is lots of mirroring or matching but the meetings that don't go so well have very little.

If you do feel you need it to bump along a bit then use the techniques above. They are much less obvious than copying someone's every movement. Don't overdo it and don't try to force it, it will happen anyway if things are going well.

If it's a meeting with more than one person, you can't mirror or match everyone anyway – you can only mirror or match one person at a time.

6
PRESENTATIONS

Studies show that the average person would rather die than do any form of public speaking. OK, not literally die, but fear of public speaking often comes out higher than fear of death. One study concluded that 53% of people would rather die than give any form of public speech.

What's so scary about presenting? For many people, it's the 'What ifs?':

- What if I go blank?

- What if the technology fails on me?

- What if they ask awkward questions?

The fact is you can't be in control of everything; you can only ever really be in control of your thoughts. Your thoughts become your feelings and your feelings show in your body language. Your job is to stay in control of your own mind and don't ever panic.

The key to presenting is pretty simple; be yourself and get your points across to your audience in the best way possible.

If you're presenting to people who know you, avoid slipping into some super 'presenter' mode, because it can backfire dramatically and you can lose credibility. It's slightly different when you are presenting to people you've never met before. In that situation you can try different ways of presenting the same material to find out what works best for you.

Once you've found out for yourself what an impact just a few simple changes have on people's perception of you, then you will have no need ever to find presentations stressful again.

Remember, presentations are about *you* first and foremost. Whatever you are trying to get across is secondary.

Body language can be an amazing ally. It can blow your audience away. Or it can ruin the best presentation you've ever written. In this chapter, you'll find out how.

DIFFERENT TYPES OF PRESENTATIONS

There are many kinds of different presentations and each brings with it its own challenges and approaches. Going into them in minute detail is beyond the scope of the book, so let's say, for the purposes of what we're trying to achieve here, that there are two types: formal and informal.

Formal

We'll call formal presentations those high-level affairs where CEOs, CFOs, board members or members of the senior management team impart information about, say, company mergers, financial results, structural changes or redundancies.

If you are the one giving a formal presentation then there are certain things you can do that will help you carry it off. It might sound a simple thing, but the number of people I've encountered at a very senior level who have no idea just how much impact a buttoned up jacket makes is incredible.

But formal presentations aren't always serious. You might be announcing some major new product or design development to the press, in which case an unbuttoned jacket adds an air of openness. Context is everything. As the presenter, you need to assess the situation and choose between gravity or something more relaxed.

Quite often, formal presentations involve some form of lectern or podium. These are great for hiding behind or as somewhere to put your notes, but they can be death when it comes to presenting. If you're short in stature you can get lost behind them – and this is even worse if there happens to be a microphone stuck in front of you as well. If at all possible, get out from behind the podium and stand either to the side or completely away from it.

Nick Clegg, now the UK's Deputy Prime Minister, did exactly this in the first of the live Prime Ministerial TV debates with David Cameron and Gordon Brown. Despite being the pre-debate underdog, the media coverage the following day gave the night to Clegg. How did he do it? Simple. For most of the hour, he stood to the side of the lectern and engaged directly with the audience in the studio and watching on TV. You could see his whole body, which you couldn't with Cameron or Brown. The message was clear: 'Look, I have nothing to hide, I stand here open and ready to engage.'

It was a serious debate, but by moving to the side he distinguished himself from his rivals.

Lecterns and podiums can be useful in other ways too. Here's another tip. If you have a mix of bad and good news to impart, stand behind it while you deliver the bad news, and move away from it to deliver the good news.

Informal

Informal presentations include all the day-to-day stuff you present to your teams, co-workers and other department staff. The thing with these types of presentations is that just about anyone can get called upon to give a little impromptu show-and-tell

It's happened to everyone: you think you're safe at the back of the room and then BAM!, you're the focus of attention.

A typical scenario for this to happen is a sales meeting where the manager calls upon you to come out to the front to tell everyone about the conversation you had with a client the other day which you managed to turn from a negative to a positive with one simple strategy.

That's it! You have to do it, you can't run and hide, the manager has just praised you in front of everyone and now is your time to shine by presenting your new strategy to your colleagues.

THE VENUE

Where your presentation takes place is critical, as there are very different considerations at work and techniques at your disposal depending on the environment you're speaking in. I'm going to focus on three typical business environments: the office, the meeting room and, most daunting of all, the stage.

1.   The office

It goes without saying that offices usually belong to someone who has some level of authority – perhaps a manager, supervisor, team leader or director. Their office will usually have their stamp all over it, as we found earlier, and there are clues and cues to take from the context when giving presentations too.

Office meetings can be short and sweet, sitting or standing, impromptu or planned. You are either the one running the meeting or you're a participant in it, and there are differences in the way you conduct yourself depending on your role.

Let's assume in the first instance that it's you who has convened the meeting, in your office, with one of your team. It doesn't matter what the topic is, it's your choice how you handle it.

Remember in the previous chapter, we talked about creating a less formal meeting space away from the main work desk? If possible, go for this set-up. Use a small, low, round table, set away from your main work desk. Desks are usually placed directly between you and anyone coming into your room, forming a huge barrier. This isn't the most conducive set-up if you want people to feel relaxed, to open up and talk freely.

Remember too, however, that in some scenarios a desk can make a useful barrier – for example, where you're dealing with under-performance, complaints and so on. Here the barrier reinforces the message. You might even want to emphasize the effect by giving them a small chair, preferably with no arm rests. This way they can't just sit and grip the chair or rest their elbows on it. They're more likely to give away unconscious signals with their body language.

If you happen to be the one called in to have a chat with your boss, then there's not usually a lot you can do to change the set-up of the office. One thing you can do is angle your chair so that it's not in a confrontational, head-on position. Sitting directly opposite someone with a big desk in the middle is generally a position you want to avoid if the other person has all the power in the relationship.

Instead, try to angle the chair in relation to them and see what effect this has. You will find the results can be quite significant.

2. The meeting room

Your standard meeting room usually contains one rectangular table surrounded by quite low-backed, identical chairs. Occasionally there is one nicer chair at the head of the table to give that position some authority.

When giving presentations in a meeting room, you can either be sat down or stood up. If you choose to present standing up, move your chair to the side or completely out of the way.

People have a habit of leaning on the back of the chair if it is just pushed in under the table. This stance puts a big barrier between you and the audience you are trying to impress. You won't impress anyone in this pose. It will make you look like you are either hiding behind it or using it as a power symbol.

Also, when you stand up, it gives you a height advantage over your audience. Height normally equals power. On its own, that's fine, but add that to standing behind a chair resting your hands on its back and the impression it gives falls into one of two extremes: either dominance or weakness, both of which you'll want to avoid.

Move the chair. It stops you from inadvertently hiding behind it or leaning on it.

3. The stage

Presenting on a stage can be a daunting prospect even for the most experienced of presenters.

If you're not experienced then it can be downright scary. All eyes are on you and you know that you have to deliver your message clearly and with enough impact that it sticks with your audience, so that they get the tone as well as the message.

Technology

Some degree of technology is normally involved and, when you are up there in front of everyone, you are not in control of it, it is merely there to aid and assist you in giving your presentation.

At the back of the room there is normally an IT professional sitting behind a control desk that wouldn't look out of place in a sci-fi film. These people can make or break your presentation, so always, always make sure you talk to whoever is responsible for the technology before you go on stage.

Make sure they know timings of absolutely everything. Give them a running order so they know when to play the video and audio clips and they play them at the right time. There is nothing worse than a piece of music or video starting up when you are still talking, or not playing at all, leaving you standing around like an idiot!

If you understand body language, you will never rely solely on technological wizardry. You will always have back-up materials so that you can pull it off even if all the technology fails.

Movement: move your audience

Apart from technology, one of the things that can kill a stage presentation is your movement – or lack of it. Too much or too little, neither is good.

Too much and you will seem nervous, stressed, even shifty. It will look as if you're not in control of your own body movements.

Too little and you will bore your audience to death.

You have to strike a balance between standing still at times and moving around at others.

The best technique for a body language expert to remember is to stand still when you are delivering the key points you want your audience to remember. Use your slides to reinforce these key points, and maximize attention on them and what you're saying, by cutting out other movement at that moment. An effective presenter understands that stillness of the body is a clever tool that can focus attention on the key points being delivered.

Once you've delivered the point, move around again and look around.

Use movement to engage and enthuse your audience. Use stillness to focus them.

Read your audience

It's important to look around at your audience and not just talk over their heads to the back of the room. You need to see how your audience is receiving what you are saying. A great presenter is not just on top of his or her own body language while giving a presentation, they are reading and responding to their audience. And you can be sure that the audience will let you know what they think.

You'll see it in their body language, nods of agreement, head shakes of rejection, sharp intakes of breath, crossing arms, hand to face gestures, positive and negative facial expressions.

These signals, movements and gestures are quite simply the life-blood of knowing whether or not you are doing a good job and getting your audience on board, or failing to take them with you.

If you can't read your audience you'll have no idea when you've finished whether the presentation you painstakingly put together thinking, 'This is going to be excellent', worked or not.

HOW TO MAKE AN IMPRESSION WHEN PRESENTING

Making a great impression is what counts when presenting. It doesn't matter if it's good news or bad, whether you're selling something or trying to get a pay rise, there are a few simple things you can employ in your own body language movements, signals and gestures that can help to influence others in a positive way towards you.

In this section I'm going to cover anchors and triggers. This is some-thing you should be using in each and every scenario covered in this book, but anchors and triggers are an especially powerful component of effective presentations, and the best presenters have an instinctive, or learned, grasp of how to use them. Anchoring Is an extremely powerful tool when set up and used correctly, so here I'll cover what it's all about and how to use it yourself any time you want.

Anchors and triggers

An anchor is designed to hold something in place for a period of time.

A trigger is designed to release something at a specific point in time.

You know that a boat or ship will use an anchor to hold the vessel in place against wind and water currents. When the captain says 'Raise the anchor', that is the trigger to release the anchor, making the craft moveable again.

That's the whole point of using anchors. In body language, anchors make a person moveable in their thinking – with a little trigger assistance from you.

When it comes to presenting, you can set up positive or negative anchors and triggers in people and fire them whenever you like.

You and everyone you know has already got thousands of anchors that are triggered by others. If you have children then you have lots of anchors the kids can fire with a look, a whimper, a sigh, a pout. Generally speaking the people you love, and love you the most, have the most anchors to trigger.

This is also true of people you believe have any form of power over you: your boss, your partner's parents, that person you told a secret to. If you think they can do you harm then chances are those same people will have anchors set in you that make you feel that way.

Anchors can be anything. You remember right at the beginning I mentioned *a particular teacher who had a funny walk when you were knee high to a grasshopper*? Well something as simple as the way someone walks can be a trigger.

If you did have a teacher with a funny walk who was a complete and utter disciplinarian then, every time you see someone with a similar walk, there is great possibility that it will trigger a memory, and even a strong emotional response. All that because of a passer-by with a funny walk.

Anchors can be very deep and triggered very easily.

Most people wander around in this world with hundreds, if not thousands, of anchors that were set up in childhood and that are triggered daily by others. Few people realize that it's these child-hood anchors that make them act like a child in adult life.

Psychological emotional anchors are powerful things and you can set them up in people deliberately to trigger whatever emotion you want them to experience when you fire it.

We've all heard someone say 'So-and-so is really pushing my but-tons' when someone is angry or frustrated. These so-called buttons are anchors that have just been triggered, and this is when most people start acting like children.

Here are just a handful of examples of anchors and triggers you can set up. It's up to you to explore all the different things you can use them for.

Touch

Touch is one of the most powerful anchors you can use and is best when connected with emotional feelings (but be careful who you touch and where!).

The wrist, forearm, upper arm, back and shoulders are all places people commonly touch, so you can start with anchoring a certain touch each time you come into contact with a specific person.

Each time you greet them you could give them a little squeeze around their upper arm, or pat them on the shoulder or back. Very soon, it will be so deeply anchored that you could do it in the dark and they would instinctively know it was you.

Another anchor which achieves the same result doesn't involve touching at all – or rather, the anchor is achieved with a specific touch movement on yourself.

Here's a scenario: if you anchor rubbing your cheek with the tip of your index finger each time someone laughs, then that action will become associated with laughter. In the future you can just rub your cheek when you say something and they'll make the association with happiness. The touch is anchored to the emotional state.

You don't have to go overboard setting up anchors. They are best kept simple so that whatever the trigger movement is doesn't become obvious or look like a nervous twitch.

Left and right hand

When presenting, a very simple anchor to set up is left and right hand movements.

CLICK 'N' STICK

One I used a lot in my selling days was the simple clicking of a pen top. I liked this one as it involved a movement and created a sound anchor. If I was presenting a product or service, each time I said something and the client responded positively, I'd verbally confirm it, 'OK, so you like that do you?' and as they answered 'Yes' I'd click the pen top and then move on.

It was both an anchor of the positives and a way of bringing a close to one part before moving on to the next topic.

Then I'd just wait until I was closing the deal and maybe felt I needed some assistance in gaining a yes. When they were 'umming and ahhing' over some point or other, I'd click the pen top and smile as I countered whatever objection they were throwing back at me. More often than not I got a yes.

Manipulative? Well, let's be realistic about it. If your product is no good, no amount of pen clicking is going to sell it. This is about using every tool at your disposal.

Give out information with your right hand moving away from your body when talking to your audience. When you want them to give you opinions and feedback for example, use your left hand by bringing it in towards your body.

You can use props too. If you're a glasses wearer, put them on when you speak and take them off when you want your audience to talk back to you, or the other way round, depending on which you prefer.

Tony Blair, former Prime Minister of the UK, uses two handed movements to such an extent that they have become synonymous with him. They are so deeply anchored that many people in a controlled test can identify him just from his hands.

He'd start a speech by using both hands moving out and away from his body whenever he was giving out information to his audience. He'd also have his fingers spread wide apart, which is an encompassing move that makes the audience feel as though you're connecting with them and sending your message to them personally.

Then, when he wanted to bring the audience with him on a certain point, he'd pull the hands in toward his chest. As he did so he'd close the wide spread fingers just like he was closing a net around the audience, bringing them in to his way of thinking.

Incidentally, Tony Blair was and is one of the most competent presenters you will ever come across. Whether or not you agree with his brand of politics is neither here nor there. When it comes to persuading people in an open forum he is one of the best in the world.

If you compare Tony Blair's presentation style with his successor Gordon Brown or *his* successor Ed Miliband, neither of them are in the same class. When they present there's very little movement. As we found earlier, lack of movement is as bad, if not worse, than too much movement. It's about striking a balance. Their hand signals are weak and they do not come across as having the conviction to back up their words.

David Cameron and Nick Clegg have styles quite similar to Tony Blair's. They both use their hands to good effect, setting up numerous anchors as they talk. They both use their facial expressions, especially the raising and lowering of eyebrows. They both use their whole body as they talk, particularly Nick Clegg.

Anchoring with other senses

There are many ways to anchor states and emotions in people. Any of your senses can be used for an anchor. Remember VAKOG? Visual, auditory, kinaesthetic, olfactory and gustatory. Everyone has had the experience of hearing a certain piece of music and immediately being transported back to your teens when that record was your absolute favourite tune. Or walking down the road and catching a waft of something in the air that takes you back to a holiday memory.

These are the five senses that pretty much govern how we interpret everything in the world. Don't try creating anchors for all of them straight off the bat. Concentrate initially on using body movements to set and trigger the anchor.

Practise them with family and friends first before you try using with clients or co-workers. But do try them out and discover just how much fun anchors are. They really can drastically change someone's emotional state in an instant.

Your anchors

Also, start to notice the various anchors other people have set up in you. If the moment you see a certain person you feel an instant shift in your emotions, whether it's happy, sad, angry, frustrated or whatever, ask yourself what it is about that person that gives you that emotion.

Chances are you will unconsciously think back to an instance in the past where they made you feel exactly the same set of emotions.

A friend of mine has a certain curling up of the right side of his lip, whenever he's annoyed at someone or something. It's his version of a snarl. His brother also has the same snarling lip. My friend's wife does not like the brother particularly so whenever the husband does it he gets an ear bashing because it reminds her of the brother.

Anchors are everywhere and everyone has them but most people don't realize they've got them, or the damage they can do in other areas of your life.

Once you start to notice the anchors that set you on a negative path, then you can start to break them and release yourself from your self-inflicted prison. Just because a particular person or situation was negative in the past does not mean it has to be now and in the future.

Not everyone who curls their snarly lip is the same as my friend's brother, so why should these anchors be true of other people? Of course, they are not.

That's why you need to form your opinions, judgements and views of people on what you see in front of you, and not base them on the past or other people's experiences.

I said at the beginning about the differences between children brought up in a safe or threatening environment and how it affects them in later life in terms of how trusting they are. The press is full of stories of old and vulnerable people being ripped off all the time. Why? Because for the most part they allow it to happen based on a false set of parameters about who is truthful and honest. The anchors that they have set up throughout their lives determine the outcomes.

Sometimes people wise up, start noticing different things, and are more cautious in a similar situation next time round. Some carry on regardless, hoping the rest of the world will change to their set of values.

The more you notice the anchors, not just in yourself but in the people around you – in how they react to triggers set off by others – the more control and influence you will have over your life and career. If you see an anchor set by someone else that triggers a reaction in someone, you too can probably use that same trigger to get the same reaction.

Just as my friend inadvertently does with his wife when he curls his lip.

Although I've given you a very in-depth look at anchors and triggers in this section, the whole idea was to make you realize how deep they go in every sort of situation. Learning to set them up and release them will always give your presentations:

1.   more impact

2.   deeper connectivity

3.   improved information retention.

SUMMARY

You are always presenting in one form or another, whether it's a one-on-one chat in the corridor or a formal presentation on a stage. You can't control everything in these situations, but what you can control is your body movements and the signals they send your audience. In this section you've hopefully learned a few simple changes that you can make to get your message across with the meaning you want and to gauge how it is received.

Use the specific left-, right- or two-handed gestures to reinforce your words, which starts to embed anchors.

Anchors are everywhere, especially in presentations. If they are not present then you are missing an opportunity to really embed your message. Everyone has them and they get triggered day in, day out by people, environments and situations.

Start to notice as many anchors as you can in yourself and break them if they have a negative effect on you. Use them more if you feel they have a positive effect on you and others.

Deliberately go about setting up new anchors in people so that you can trigger them at a later stage when you want to change or influence their emotional state.

7

SALES AND NEGOTIATIONS

We are all selling all the time, so let's look at how understanding body language can help in sales and negotiation situations.

Selling a product, service or concept is about getting the buyer to the point where they want whatever it is you are trying to sell them. Once you get to that point, you enter the negotiation phase.

Very few buyers after seeing and hearing your pitch will say, 'Ok, where do I sign?' It does happen but not that often.

You've got to have done the selling part right or you never get to negotiation. All of the body language you've learned in this book up to now, your greetings, meetings, presentations and all the rest, make up the selling part. Once you've got through that successfully, you get to the point where a price for said product, service or concept is on the table, and that's where negotiation starts.

Well that's what most sales people believe anyway!

Negotiating actually started before you even entered the building. You or someone from your company probably spoke to them to book the initial appointment. If so, you or a telesales person did an initial quick sales presentation over the phone and then arranged a time for both parties to meet. If you book your own appointments, I thoroughly recommend you start negotiating immediately.

Let's assume you're speaking to a potential buyer and they agree to see you. They say, 'I can see you on Thursday at 4pm'. Don't just jump straight on it and agree. Try to get it shifted an hour, a day, a week, by replying with something like, 'Ahh, I've got another meeting that may go over time so rather than be late can we shift it back an hour?'

Why would you do that? To be a pain in the neck? No. This immediately gives you insight into how flexible they are. Listen to the changes in voice tones and body movements.

Yes, you *can* hear body movements over the phone. Obviously you can't actually see what they are doing but you can definitely pick up when someone sighs or breathes in quickly, when they move around, maybe whether they're walking while talking, out in the open, in an office, if there are other people around. If you pick up that they're in a good mood then try to negotiate. You can always agree to Thursday 4pm if you don't think they'll play ball.

So let's assume you agreed a time and you're now sat with your prospective client. You've been through your range of new skills; you've done the greeting, wandered along to a meeting room and you're engaged in the presenting, selling and negotiating part of your job.

You can read your future client's thinking processes by observing and decoding what their eye movements are telling you.

THE EYES AND EYE CONTACT

People have all sorts of preconceived ideas about what you can and can't tell from a person's eyes and eye movements. It's not surprising when you consider that we grow up hearings lots of clichés, phrases and sayings used in everyday situations.

- 'If looks could kill'

- 'Did you see their beady little eyes?'

- 'Beauty is in the eye of the beholder'

- 'The eyes are the window of the soul'

- 'You never know how you look through other people's eyes'. (The Johari window!)

There are dozens more but, setting aside all the clichés, phrases and sayings, which for the most part do have a semblance of truth in them, let me now open your eyes to the truth. According to a study researching memory by Wharton University this is a breakdown of information processed through the different channels.

- Eyes 82%

- Ears 11%

- Other senses (touch, taste and smell) 7%.

As they were researching memory, they were also looking at how much information people remember if they see it as well as hear it and came to this conclusion.

- Retention: verbal   10%

- Retention: verbal and visual   51%.

In other words, if you use visual input as well as verbal, people will remember more. In fact, over five times more.

- It's why companies spend thousands on logos and branding.

- It's why you use laptops and projectors when giving larger presentations.

- It's why almost every company of any note on the planet has some form of brochure, leaflet or sticker.

Visual input is important. It's what observing body language is all about; picking up on the unspoken elements of a meeting, presentation or negotiation. If you are going to use visual aids then make sure that they are clean, presentable and working as you expect them to.

So, if we take in all this information through our eyes, how much do we give out?

Studies using tiny cameras embedded in pictures or within specially adapted glasses have shown where the eyes actually focus most of their attention when looking at someone's face.

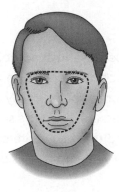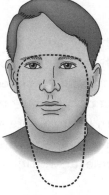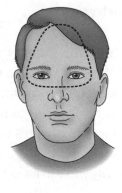

Sociable gaze   Extended gaze   Assertive gaze

Sociable gaze

This is roughly a small triangle from one eye to the other and down to the nose, mouth or chin and is seen most often when people are getting on well. You probably have your own favourite spot to look at on someone's face when you interact with them, start noticing where you actually look and it will give you an idea of how you come across to others.

Extended gaze

This is roughly the same as above but just goes beyond the chin and generally it doesn't go any lower than the chest. If you see someone looking at you below that level a lot, then maybe they know something you don't. It's certainly a more analytical gaze and for sure could even indicate physical attraction – literally checking you out.

Assertive gaze

This is the opposite of the sociable gaze because instead going from the eyes down to the nose, mouth or chin it goes up to the forehead. Try this on anyone and within seconds you normally get a reaction. It seems to put people under pressure. Keep the same blinking rate or you'll turn it into a stare and that can invite confrontation. Again it's your choice as to when you employ this one. Certainly you can have some fun with it!

EYE ACCESSING CUES

I mentioned eye accessing cues briefly in the section on YODA. It's the O in Observation. Eye accessing cues are an area of neuro linguistic programming (NLP). It relates to how your eyes tend to move up, down, left, right and around the whole 360 degrees that they can rotate, when you talk, listen, think, visualize, and so on.

You see people moving their eyes around all the time but, have you ever noticed that they tend to go in the same direction for certain information? Well, they do.

What it is

NLP was created by two guys from completely different backgrounds, John Grinder and Richard Bandler. One was a linguist, the other a psychologist. They worked together in the early 1970s studying human behaviour patterns. After watching numerous interactions between clients and eminent therapists in their fields such as Fritz Perls, Virgina Satir and Milton Erickson, whose work is still used to this day in many areas of psychiatry and psychotherapy, they noticed that with most people there is a specific pattern or sequence of directions in which the eyes move when processing or recalling certain groups of information. This pattern of behaviour they came up with became known as 'eye accessing cues'.

What this means is that the eyes have noticeable direction cues when accessing the brain to process or recall information. Let me enlighten you as to where they go for what information – with the caveat that this is just the usual state of affairs, and doesn't cover *every* instance.

How it works

There are essentially six main areas in which the eyes can move. Understanding this map will give you a good basic understanding of eye accessing cues.

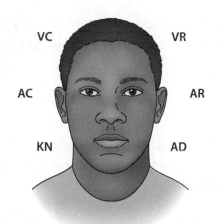

VC Visual construction	**VR** Visual recall
AC Auditory constructed	**AR** Auditory remembered
KN Kinaesthetic	**AD** Auditory dialogue

1.   *VC (visual construction):* This is the direction your eyes go to create visual images and also to analyze and process numerical information.

2.   *VR (visual recall):* When your eyes go in this direction, they are recalling visual images of things that have actually happened and are being pictured in the mind.

3.   *AC (auditory constructed):* This is the direction your eyes go to imagine new sounds.

4.   *AR (auditory remembered):* When your eyes go in this direction they are accessing memories of sound.

5.   *AD (auditory dialogue):* This is also referred to as AID or ID, the (I) standing for internal – your eyes tend to go in this direction when having an internal conversation or being careful.

6.   *KN (kinaesthetic):* This is the direction most people's eyes go when processing or thinking about emotions and feelings.

How to use it

Using eye accessing cues is a simple matter of watching the direction a person's eyes go when you ask or talk about certain things. So what's the point?

Well, it can be used to understand how someone is thinking from moment to moment. It can help you work out whether someone is being deceptive. It can be used to see how someone is processing information.

Here's a brief list of sample questions. Try it on yourself – you'll be amazed. It really works.

- VC: How would it look if we were to install the equipment on the third floor?

- VR: Can you picture the chaos caused last time your computers crashed?

- AC: Can you imagine what our competitors are going to say?

- AR: What was all that noise outside the meeting room?

- AD: If your mentor was here what would they say?

- KN: How do you feel about the merger now it's going through?

Remember this is only a guide, it is *not* an absolute. People think differently. That's why the safest way to use it is to establish a base-line of which direction they go by asking a series of related questions. When you can see a definite pattern then you can use it in other ways.

Remember:

- Some people are the complete opposite.

- Some people don't have a pattern.

- Some people move all over the place.

- Some people just look straight ahead.

- It's not set in stone so practise – even if you don't want to use it, just watch in which direction people move their eyes for the fun of it.

LYING AND DECEPTION

Once you've established someone's pattern for processing certain information it can also be used quite effectively to check whether someone is telling the truth.

If, for example, they always look up and to the left whenever they recall a visual memory you can question them about a particular scene and notice whether their eyes stay checking the information up and to the left or whether they suddenly shift to the other side, which would indicate it's not a memory but possibly a made up piece of information.

Now, the nature of selling and negotiating means that a sales person doesn't always tell the whole truth and neither do many negotiators. It's a game of bluff, with the seller trying to retain as much profit in the deal as they can, and the negotiator trying to save as much money as possible for their company.

Sales and negotiating is a game of smoke and mirrors. I don't know how many times in my career I've been told by a buyer; 'XYZ is our absolute bottom line'. Yet when all the haggling is over they've paid more than that and been happy to do so.

An element of deception is part of the game. Whether it's a one-man 'Fred in a Shed' business or a huge multimillion-dollar corporation, they all keep things back from the end customer. Not for malicious reasons but for sheer commercial sense.

Lying and deception is another specialist area so I've brought in Drew McAdam, an ex-army interrogator, to add a little more detail and give you a fuller picture of liars and the process of lying.

LIES, ALL LIES (DREW MCADAM)

There is a generally held view that with a modicum of training it's possible to spot when somebody is lying, and to recognize deceit with unfailing accuracy. If only it were that simple.

Unfortunately, the truth about lying is much more complicated. A little bit of knowledge is a dangerous thing. Just because somebody displays a deceit 'tell', such as scratching their nose, it would be a mistake to draw the conclusion that they are fibbing. They may just have an itchy nose.

Of course, study and practice all help, but no matter how highly trained you might be, it's worth bearing in mind that it is possible to make a fundamental error.

More important than deception recognition is using questioning techniques that cut to the heart of the matter. Such techniques and skills are taught at The Army School of Service Intelligence.

Getting confessions is one thing, but perhaps more useful in business and personal life is the area of 'tactical questioning'. This helps the questioner recognize through the body language the exact moment when somebody reacts negatively to a statement or a question even though they try to mask or deny it.

This ability to observe and recognize an emotional shift at the exact moment it happens, is relatively simple once you understand *why* it happens. It is then just a matter of working out why your statement or question produced such an effect.

The good news is, once you understand why people react to stress and what these reactions are, it's a simple task to put it to good use.

A QUICK LOOK AT THE BRAIN

To understand what our body does and why it does it, we have to take a quick look at the brain.

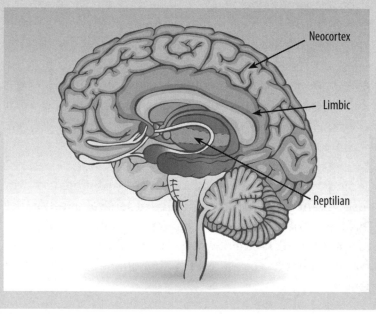

- Reptilian brain – this keeps the organs of the body going, regulating everything from temperature to breathing and heart rate.
- Limbic system – this area deals with emotions. Its job is to learn from experience then to use that experience to avoid pain, pursue pleasure and regain emotional stability.
- Neocortex – this is the 'modern' brain and is the centre of higher mental functions in humans. It is the part of the brain which does not simply act and react to stimuli but is under conscious control.

Imagine several hunters have been out tracking bears all day, night has fallen, they are deep in the woods, round a campfire, sipping coffee and chatting. Suddenly, there is a rustle in the bushes and the crack of a twig. First reaction? Everybody freezes. Time stops. The decision is made. Fight or flight… that is the limbic system at work. It reacts to the perceived threat, then demands action be taken. This all happens instantly, instinctively and at a subconscious level. You have absolutely no control over it.

We can understand why hunters in a dark wood would react to the sound of a cracking twig, but in everyday life the limbic system reacts to any disagreeable experience in exactly the same way, whether it be in a car salesroom, classroom, the boardroom, or in your own home. Anything that creates stress or concern will alert the limbic system. However, the important thing to understand is that in the very moment the stress is created, a powerful part of the brain does more than just react; it also demands instant pacification.

Now, instead of the hunters in the wood, let's take the example where Joe from the post room has taken the day off claiming he is sick. The following day he turns up at work and his boss calls him into the office for a word.

'I called you at home yesterday afternoon but there was no answer, where were you?'

'That's strange. I was in bed all day – are you sure you called the right number?'

Now, while the answer is reasonable – maybe even quite clever – if the boss is smart he will not be listening to Joe's words but watching for signs that the limbic system is under stress. In the very moment the question is asked, Joe's brain goes through exactly the same process as that experienced by the hunters. The limbic system doesn't know or care whether it's possible danger from a bear in a bush or an awkward question from the boss. The anxiety, stress, and concern causes the limbic system to send out a demand to be placated. In that moment, Joe will do something to meet the brain's demand.

What he will do depends on Joe, and what works for him. We are all different and the pacifying behaviours we demonstrate will vary from person to person. However, there are some common pacifying reactions – or 'adapters' as they are more correctly known.

The fastest way to placate the brain's internal turmoil is to flood it with endorphins. The quickest way to do that is to stimulate nerve endings. In my time I have had a few house-hold pets and, without exception, I discovered that gently stroking an animal below the jaw will cause it to relax. The stimulation of the nerves in that area produces a rush of en-dorphins to the brain. So, we shouldn't be surprised to see Joe stroke the fleshy area at the front of the throat, perhaps even tug at the skin. This is a classic adapter, one you will see often – and now you know why the person is doing it.

When being questioned under pressure the person answer-ing may rub the side of their neck. This is an area where you can find the carotid sinus, within which there are barorecep-tors that respond to stimulation by reducing blood pressure.

Another area that people under stress will caress is the jugular notch or suprasternal notch. This is the hollow at the bottom of the throat where it meets the top of the sternum. This is more common with females, sometimes disguised as playing with a necklace or pendant. Males tend to tug the fleshy area at the front of the throat, just above the Adam's Apple.

Let's assume you are running through a list of conditions in a contract and the potential client is telling you he is happy with them but raises his hand and tugs the skin at his throat when you read through Clause 4. You have just hit a barrier, something that could easily derail the sales process.

He may say he is happy with the price/delivery date or what-ever, but he isn't. His limbic system has been alerted to some-thing that concerns him and is demanding to be soothed.

With that knowledge you can now spend a bit more time on Clause 4 and uncover any concerns.

The beauty with this is that there is no time delay. It happens in real time. As you read out Clause 4, the reaction takes place at that exact instant.

Of course, it doesn't have to be a contract. It might be a series of questions you are asking. Going back to Joe, the lad from the post room, the questions might go along the lines of asking how long he has been with the company, if he enjoys his work, and then: 'So, just how ill were you yesterday?'

Now, Joe may not pull at the fleshy part of his throat but if his limbic system is in turmoil, he will generally do *something*.

The signs of deception

Now let me give you some of the most common signs of deception.

- *Micro expressions* – these are quite common when it comes to lying. They flash across the face very quickly and are replaced by the emotion the person thinks you want to see.

- *Fake or fixed smiles* – the emotion behind them is not genuine so the zygomatic and orbicularis oculi muscles (see Chapter 4) don't work together in the same way as a genuine smile, which reach from the corners of the mouth to the corners of the eyes.

- *Fidgety legs, foot shaking, crossing and uncrossing the legs, raising the heels or toes up off the ground* – the legs and feet are furthest from the brain and so are consequently harder to consciously control.

- *Prolonged eye contact or broken eye contact* – people tend to react in one of two ways with their eyes and will either break the eye contact as they feel uncomfortable telling the lie or they will have a prolonged gaze, as if to say 'Challenge me if you dare'. The normal blinking rate is around 20–25bpm but that will often increase or decrease when someone tells lies.

- *Any form of self-assurance gestures* – things like rubbing the back or side of neck, bringing hands up to the face often particularly around the nose and mouth area, licking the lips often too as the mouth dries up when under pressure or telling lies.

There are many more signs of deception. Get used to spotting these and others will stand out too. Look for gestures that are incongruent with normal behaviour patterns or the words the person is using.

SUMMARY

In this chapter we've covered a lot of information on the eyes and eye contact, and looked at how exactly you use your eyes to go fetch information from your brain.

Eye contact is a crucial part of an interaction and is a good indicator of how the relationship is moving along at any point in time.

You've also learned how to use your eye contact to put pressure on others with the assertive gaze and when others may be looking at you in a more analytical way.

If you add to that the information on eye accessing cues you start to get a much clearer picture of the person you are dealing with, how they feel, where they go for information. This, as you've also learned, can be useful in spotting deception or someone being evasive.

You should now understand the connection between the words someone uses and the sense they use to process their thoughts – VAKOG. In sales your job is to sell feelings; it is the feeling 'peace of mind' you are selling, nothing else. By using the buyer's senses you allow them to engage at a much deeper level, to attain peace of mind and to reassure them that they are making the right decision to buy your product, service or idea.

8

AGGRESSION, CONFRONTATION, TERRITORY AND PROPERTY

The body language of aggression and confrontation can be quite frightening. Fortunately, most anger doesn't actually spill over into physical violence in the workplace. However, aggression and confrontation is common in the work environment.

If you work in a restaurant, bar, nightclub, the security industry or any place where you deal with the general public in a service capacity, chances are you've experienced bullying of some sort. Even if you don't work in these environments you'll probably have come across bullying in some form.

A book on body language wouldn't be complete without reference to the negative situations we sometimes find ourselves in. In this chapter, I'll cover personal space, body types, verbal consistency and congruence, and bullying.

THE POMODORO

People don't always mean to get aggressive. Sometimes you simply don't realize how your body language affects others. Then there are those who know exactly what they are doing and do it deliberately to get their own way. Maybe I was doing that on this occasion.

Those of you that like Italian food or speak the language will know exactly what *pomodoro* means, it's Italian for tomato, but in this instance it's also the name of a restaurant I frequented in Sharm El Sheikh, Egypt, when on holiday. I'd heard lots about this restaurant, all good, so decided to visit with my family while there, but our first experience there was not a good one.

The reason I mention this now is that Safwat, the manager, had the dubious pleasure of dealing with me as a very disgruntled and unhappy customer some years back. I was complaining, but without realizing it I was also trying to bully.

My family and I had ordered, didn't get our drinks, the food was late, dishes weren't hot enough, didn't get what we ordered, etc. A whole series of genuine reasons for a customer to be a bit upset.

Safwat, a man who'd been running restaurants all his life, and dealt with the odd angry customer in his time, was absolutely brilliant. No matter what I said or how scary I looked with my wild flailing arms and hand gestures, he simply kept control by nodding in agreement in all the right places. His smile was so disarming that it completely diffused my anger.

If Safwat had been looking around the restaurant while I was complaining and not focused on my complaints, then his words would have meant nothing. You can't separate words from their context. It's the combination of the words *and* the body language that gives the real meaning of the interaction. You can say 'I love you too' meaningfully to a loved one or totally sarcastically to someone getting on your nerves. Same words, different meaning. Safwat's humble body posture, pleadingly disarming smile, bowing of head and shrugging shoulders all served a purpose and that was simply to calm me down.

I'm going to cover verbal consistency and congruence shortly but, before that, I have to admit that his next move would have been to call someone to remove me from his restaurant or escort me out himself, had his efforts to calm things not worked. They did though and I appreciated them.

It was because of this man's absolute professionalism that my family gave Pomodoro another chance. As it happened, we went back again and again and got the type of service we should have got on the first visit. We became friends with Safwat and his head chef. After that, we were treated like celebrities whenever we returned.

Although the words are not what I'm talking about here, they have to be matched with consistent body language. If they aren't then people instinctively believe what they see not what they hear. That's why so many people get a hunch, gut feeling, sixth sense that something just isn't right. They can't put their finger on it, but something they've observed unconsciously sends up a warning signal.

How many times have you heard people say, 'I knew there was something wrong but I just didn't go with my instincts'?

Whenever you find yourself in a position where you feel negative or uncomfortable yet everything is seemingly positive, ask yourself what it is that doesn't stack up. Chances are you'll find that the words someone is using aren't matched by their body movements. They're out of sync, or the facial expressions are wrong or incomplete.

SPACE INVADERS

We have lots of verbal expressions for these non-verbal actions; being too pushy, stand-offish, shifty, overbearing, in-your-face, up close and personal. These terms invariably refer to our personal space and territory.

If someone invades your personal space it usually makes you lean back away from them, unless you feel comfortable with that person. If it's really uncomfortable you'll physically step backwards. 'On the back foot' is another expression commonly used.

Space invaders was one of the first arcade games I ever played, in my local chip shop when I was 16, but it's also a term that's come to mean 'people who make others feel uncomfortable by simply being too close to them physically and invading their personal space'.

We've all come across them. They just have to be right up close and personal to everyone they interact with.

Everyone has zones around their body in which they allow certain people and not others. If anyone breaks into these zones it sets off internal alarm bells or the fight-or-flight instinct.

Each of these zones is meant for different people in different situations. One minute you allow someone into your space and the next you won't. It's incredibly complex, but totally instinctive.

A typical loving relationship is the perfect example of how the same zones are available and open one minute and completely shut down the next.

You get all loved up with your partner but at the critical moment you say something you shouldn't. All of a sudden the bodies separate, the shutters go down and you're not allowed into that zone anymore. Not till you've done some grovelling!

The movement in and out or coming together of personal space is a good indicator of interest, trust and sociability, so look out for it; it happens constantly.

SPATIAL ZONES

Everybody has their own personal space around their body and will react instinctively if any particular area is encroached upon by those with whom you do not hold a certain level of relationship. Earlier, in Chapter 1, I mentioned Edward T. Hall and proxemics: these are the five zones he formulated and the relationship status needed to be allowed in to any one particular area.

- Close intimate zone: 0–15 cm / 0–6 inches

- Intimate zone: 15–45 cm / 6–18 inches

- Personal zone: 45 cm–1.2 m / 18 inches–4 feet

- Social zone: 1.2 m–3.6 m / 4–12 feet

- Public zone: 3.6 m or 12 feet and over – seminars, presentations, etc.

Close intimate zone

The close intimate zone is reserved for very special people, your close family and friends, children and pets. If anyone else tries to get that close to you, you pull back and away from them physically, maybe even turn your face or, in extreme cases, turn your back on them.

Intimate zone

The intimate zone is just a little further from the body but is still very close. Again there are only certain people you are going to let that close and still feel comfortable with. Mainly friends, children and animals again.

Personal zone

The personal zone is that comfortable distance you stand from someone when you're chatting in social scenarios but it's also the acceptable distance for workplace interactions. Any closer and you could be seen as overbearing.

Social zone

The social zone is not exactly what it would appear. Social in this context means people you deal with that you don't really know, where you want to keep just a little bit of extra distance between you: a plumber visiting your home to fix a burst pipe, for example. Shop counters keep customer and server about this distance apart.

Public zone

The public zone is everything else outside the other four zones. It's where we tend to keep people when giving speeches, doing big presentations and so on. It's the natural distance for your audience. Any closer and you talk over the front few rows, any further and it becomes impersonal.

It should be noted that these zones were derived from studies in mainly urban, English-speaking areas, and vary massively according to culture. Generally, the more densely populated the area you were brought up in, the closer you are used to being to other people. If you were brought up on a farm in the middle of Nowhereville, then your personal zones are likely to be much bigger than your city dwelling counterpart.

Density of population to land area seems to be the dominant factor. Japan, for example, has approximately twice the population of the UK with around 120 million people living in roughly the same land mass area of the UK, which has only 60 million. Consequently, most people in Japan are quite tightly packed together throughout their lives. They even have *oshiya* on the subway. These are people whose job it is to physically push people onto the train to cram as many in as possible.

Actually, *oshiya* is also an example of one of those situations where people will let complete strangers touch them. You will allow strangers to touch you, but only in certain circumstances, like on public transport. Even then they're only allowed to touch in certain areas of your body; your back and shoulders and your arms, but not your hands or fingers. If a stranger goes to touch the front of your body, you will react in an instant.

Space is a key area of body language so pay attention to it. Play around with it too. It's great fun watching people react instantly to you moving into their intimate or personal zones! It's also a good way of finding out who finds you attractive and/or trustworthy.

TERRITORY

Essentially we are all animals and, just like most animals, we have territories we claim as our own. People claim all sorts of things as theirs whether they are or not. A parking space outside their house, a favourite seat on the train. I bet you've got your favourite chair at home and no one's allowed to sit in it when you're in the house.

Invade someone's territory at your own risk. It's like the physical space around them but now extended to inanimate, material things as well. People touch and lean on things they claim as theirs or regard as being in their territory.

If a salesperson knocks on your door at home, chances are you will lean against your door frame or have your hand and arm leaning on the open door itself.

Leaning on things can also be a sign of intransigence. If you're chatting away with someone and say something they disagree with, their response may be to grip the back of a chair or lean on it. All of a sudden it's become a 'taking a stance' signal.

I mentioned at the beginning about the three environments where you spend most of your time, but it goes beyond that. We regularly claim things that aren't really ours. You just assume them as your property or territory. Human beings aren't property, but in photographs of couples you will often see ownership signals where one or both are touching the other.

Look out for these property and territory display signals. They are an instant indicator of how someone is feeling – but, as with all body language, read all the signs not just one element.

Leaning on a chair back, for example, could demonstrate that the person is feeling perfectly comfortable with the situation, or it may be that they're using it as a barrier. If it's all smiles and laughter then chances are it's not a barrier signal but one of comfort or belonging.

However, if the atmosphere had just become frosty because of something you or someone else has said, then it's probably a barrier. The facial expressions and conversation will be the determining factors here.

Context, and reading the entire story, is everything with body language.

HEIGHT, SIZE AND SHAPE

Up to now I've not really made much reference to your physical height and size, but it has an impact, a big impact, on how people perceive you. It's one of those stereotypes people hold dear and use as their own quick reference guide.

- If you happen to be overweight, a lot of people naturally assume you are also unfit and lazy.

- If you happen to be extremely thin, people think you've got eating problems.

- If you're very tall, people can be intimidated by your height without you saying a word.

- If you are very short, people often feel they can treat you like a little kid.

- If you happen to be one of the four above then you've probably encountered this many times over.

A person's height and size are one of the first things the world sees, so it has an impact on that first impression. Consequently, lots of people who are overweight, thin, very tall or short, will often try to compensate because they know all the stereotypes. There are others, of course, who use their height and size to their advantage.

Your body type

According to an NHS study of 2009, the average English man is 5ft 9ins (1.75m) tall and weighs 13.2st (185lbs/83.9kg). The average woman is 5ft 3½ins (1.62m) tall and weighs 11st (155lbs/70.2kg).

There are many factors that determine your adult height and physical size, with your genes, diet and exercise being the main building blocks for your body shape.

There are three body shapes.

- Endomorph – shorter rounded body shape with weight centrally distributed.

- Mesomorph – wide hips and shoulders, slimmer waist, evenly proportioned.

- Ectomorph – typically of slim build, long legs and small body frame.

Just because there are only three body shapes doesn't mean you are only one of them. If you have a tall slim father and a short rotund mother you'll probably be a mix of the two, an Ectoendomorph.

Or maybe you're an Endomesomorph, in which case you'll typically be tall with a big, athletic build. Or you might be an Ectoendomorph and carry all your weight up top with slim legs.

Your body shape has an influence over the clothes you wear too. Tall people often have sleeves that are too short, short people have material bunched up at the bottom of their trousers.

Overweight people can look bound up in their clothes whereas skinny people can look like their clothes just hang on them.

All these things have an influence on how you look and, whilst the way you look is not the be-all and end-all in business, it counts for a lot, especially first impressions. Get that wrong and you may not be given a second chance.

There's not much you can do about your body shape but there is lots you can do to make the best of what you've got. It's not just about the clothes you wear, it's also how you use your physical size and shape.

Generally speaking, when in confrontational situations you will either try to make yourself look bigger to stand your ground, or you'll collapse inwards making yourself appear smaller, weaker and more submissive.

This happens all the time, though not just in confrontational situations. Making yourself bigger or smaller is a non-verbal sign telling you whether or not someone agrees with what's being said or done. It's a little like when someone leans in and out in a conversation. It's an indicator of where they are emotionally.

For example, I mentioned earlier about sitting with your elbows out resting on the arms of the chair making you look bigger and confident, or tucking your elbows in, making yourself smaller and more submissive. Well, you can use both when you want to play both roles, which in business meetings is quite often. One minute you might need to make people take notice. Other times you'll want to sink into your chair and hope you don't get noticed at all.

Keep your eyes open to other people using their size in this way.

People use height and size to bully others too. They don't always know they're doing it, or mean to do it, but they do.

Standing over someone sitting in a chair means there's a massive height difference, especially if the person standing is tall as well. This can be very dominant. If you add to that a question from the standing person said with just a slightly frustrated voice tone and you have a very intimidating set-up. You see this going on during business encounters day in, day out.

When you want to make yourself bigger, just breathe in to your full lung capacity, which will puff out your chest, then just square off your shoulders. Conversely, if you want to look smaller, breathe out as much as you can, take small breaths, collapse your shoulders inwards and lower your head slightly.

You can do this sitting or standing – it has same effect.

VERBAL CONSISTENCY AND CONGRUENCE

Body language adds colour to verbal communication. I know some people use very colourful words anyway, but I'm not talking about that, I'm talking about people's attitudes, emotions, and feelings towards different people, environments and situations.

You can't separate the words being used from the actual body movements, signals and gestures – they're all wrapped up together. While the verbal language is being spoken, the body is reacting to internal and external stimuli.

If the body language is consistent with the words then all is essentially good. It's when the words don't match what the body is saying that you have to question what's going on.

Let's assume you're the boss talking to one of your staff about upcoming changes to the shift patterns and workers. You go through it explaining why the company is doing it and then get to the bit where you talk about who they are going to be working with. As you mention one name you see a momentary grimace on their face, immediately replaced by an incomplete smile that doesn't reach the eyes. This is a micro expression of fear.

In an instant, your employee has told you they don't like a certain person and don't relish the task of working with them. At this point, you as the boss have a choice. You're now armed with the knowledge to make a decision with confidence. Understanding body language is all about giving you choices about how you handle any given situation.

You can question the person to find out why they reacted the way they did, in which case they either tell you the truth or they might well lie to you. By the time you reach the end of this book, you should have a very good idea of when someone is lying.

Armed with the knowledge that employee X doesn't like employee Y, you may well change their shift so the two never have to clash. Let's face it, nothing destroys businesses faster than staff who can't get on. Things just don't get done on time or properly while people are playing mind games at work.

Obviously you can just ignore it, but that could well lead to that staff member leaving or constantly being off sick to avoid confrontation. If that happens, you have to recruit more staff, which costs time and money, especially if training is required.

You work with these people day in, day out, so you should already have a very good idea of their patterns, mood shifts, displays of emotions and attitudes. Don't ignore them or you may regret it.

It's taking notice of people's everyday behaviours (YODA) that will tell you if they are being consistent when you talk to them. It's more difficult when you are dealing with new people all the time as you have no baselines. Baseline behaviour is important as it gives you an idea of how they are likely to react, but it's not essential. Human beings have fairly standard reactions to things and show them in much the same ways. Usually the only difference is the extent of the reactions shown in their body movements and signals.

BULLYING

We're getting into a specialist area here – and hopefully not an area you'll ever have to deal with yourself – but understanding how body language is used by bullies, and can be used *against* bullies, is incredibly powerful. My friend Mark McKenzie wrote the following piece specifically for this book.

Mark is known as Mr Bullyproof and teaches clients how to handle bullies. His job is to deal with bullying in the workplace. Here's what he has to say.

How to deal with bullies (Mark McKenzie)

Reading the body language of my clients is essential for me to help them to solve their bullying problems.

It is important to gain as much useful information from my clients as I can and I've found that I learn more from *how* they tell me what their problems are than *what* they tell me.

When describing what somebody does to them they will often adopt a posture which looks uncomfortable and this is frequently the very posture they use when they are being bullied.

In these cases, I am able to see what the bully sees and I have some perspective of how the bully is able to dominate, control or otherwise hurt them. Bullies read body language just as well as everyone else.

They are able to see just how well their bullying tactics are working and, over time, learn to hone their skills and perfect whatever type of manipulation will work on their victim. My job is to teach them how to change the way they physically react in order to change the way their body language communicates with the bully.

Sometimes, all I need to do is change the way in which they sit or stand when somebody attempts to bully them, which immediately removes the impact of words or actions that previously were hurtful.

This goes beyond pure body language, because it actually changes the way they feel, even when the same things are being done to them; because the hurt is gone their body language will naturally alter and the bully will take notice.

When the bully reads this new body language they will realize that their tactics are no longer working and that they will have to change their own behaviour.

Here are two case studies of clients of mine who were being bullied in the workplace and needed to use body language to solve their problems. All names have been changed to ensure anonymity.

Case Study 1: Jayne

Jayne had a problem with one of her co-workers, Richard, who was overbearing and dominant in his interactions with Jayne. He would tell her what to do and never ask advice or give her the respect that he should as his equal. Jayne became very frustrated with him, and often tried to tell him that his behaviour wasn't appropriate for their working relationship, but he would make excuses in order to justify his actions and continue making demands. Jayne became exhausted with these conversations and, more often than not, would give in for 'an easier life'.

I wanted to know how they were positioned in the office relative to each other. They sat side by side, with a small partition

between their desks, still allowing them to see each other clearly.
I also needed to know how she sat at her desk when he started
telling her what to do. She sat with her chair far back so that she
was perched on the very front of her seat, and lent on her desk
with her shoulders and head far forward and her face very close
to the monitor. When I asked why she sat like this she said it was
so that she could only see the monitor and that everything else
(especially Richard) was completely out of sight. To her, if she
couldn't see him, then he wasn't there. Asked how she felt in this
position, she said that she felt safe.

It was important for me to show Jayne some perspective on how
her body language looked to Richard, so I mimicked her own
posture and asked her to tell me whether it looked safe or not.
She said 'not at all, it looks really vulnerable'.

She instantly had the realization that the posture she had
adopted to hide away from Richard looked submissive and pos-
sibly even invited the bullying behaviour.

We then did some role play, still with me as her and her as Rich-
ard, where I used a variety of different postures and she had to
make demands of me. With each one, we discussed how it felt
for her to give a demand, and we chose her favourite postures to
install into her body language.

The most effective one (i.e. the posture in which it was most dif-
ficult to dominate) involved her sitting right back in the chair
with her back straight using the backrest for support, with loose
muscles and feeling relaxed. Her chair was now much closer to
her desk.

When I, as Richard, issued a demand she had to swivel her chair to give me her full attention, with her head upright and her arms using the full length of the armrests with palms down. She then had to pause deliberately to consider her response before answering slowly and concisely. Having her head tilted would give a signal of listening and considering, in comparison to her upright head showing full acknowledgement yet subtle defiance.

My feedback from Jayne is that these small changes in body language completely altered Richard's interaction with her. He still asks her to do things but now is polite and respectful. When she does choose to help him out with one of his requests, he is grateful. There is now more equality between them, and although we also did some work on the verbal communication she uses, she tells me that it is the body language that made the biggest difference.

Case Study 2: David

David was struggling in business meetings. He was feeling completely left out in meetings with clients because his colleague, Graham, would exclude him from the conversation. Graham would regularly talk over David, finish sentences for him, and answer questions that the clients directed at David. David felt that Graham was embarrassing him in front of the clients but felt that he could do nothing about it during the meeting for fear of appearing unprofessional. When he tried to address the situation after the meetings, Graham would suggest that the meeting had gone well and the client was happy so there wasn't a problem. David felt increasingly alienated, both from Graham and from the clients he was supposed to be looking after.

I asked David to show me their positions during the meeting: where he, Graham and the client sat relative to each other. Graham would sit down first, square on to the client. David had a habit of sitting beside Graham with his chair a little further away from the client. Immediately, it was obvious to me who was going to lead the meeting, and who chose to take the back seat. In this position, David could not easily attract eye contact from either Graham or the client and it would be difficult for him to interject. It would be almost as if he were interrupting someone else's conversation. More often than not, when the client posed a question, they would automatically direct it at Graham even if it was in David's area of expertise.

Next, I wanted to know how both Graham and David sat and how they moved as they spoke. David imitated Graham to show me how he behaved. Graham would sit upright in his chair, his back away from the backrest, taking up a lot of room with his arms and legs splayed wide. His arms were held up and forwards as he spoke, creating an imaginary channel between him and the client, whilst physically blocking David. His head was upright and his feet flat on the floor. In contrast, David's own posture during a meeting consisted of sitting on the edge of his seat, prominently leaning forward and having to lift his head in order to face the others. His elbows were tight into his sides and his fists were clenched. His feet were positioned under the seat with his heels off the ground.

My solution for David was for him to wait for Graham and the client to sit first, then move a chair into 'referee position': directly between and to the side of them. He was to sit upright in a similar posture to Graham. He was to use his hands to direct the conversation. When he wanted to interject, he was to lift one hand slightly with index finger towards the ceiling, indicating that the others should give him attention. By offering a hand forwards with palm up, he could suggest an idea and immediately gain the attention of either of the others. I wanted David to feel like the chairman of a political debate. He could use these hand gestures to direct the meeting. Moreover, alongside his positioning, the hand gestures would invite the others to look for his involvement. In addition, I encouraged David to speak more slowly and clearly to give his voice the same authority that his body language was exhibiting.

This worked well for David. To begin with, Graham seemed very unhappy with the changes he had made but within a couple of weeks he willingly gave David the respect that he wanted. With David assuming authority during meetings, Graham would consequently have felt as though he were losing his, and therefore was encouraged to seek a state of equality between them.

I have never had a client where I have not found it useful to train them in body language skills. Additionally, I use my own body language to gain rapport and positively influence them. There is a massive difference between simply giving advice, which generally isn't effective, and physically training someone how to respond. It is the difference between knowing what to do and applying knowledge in order to make changes happen. With their new-found body language skills and a few changes in attitude, my clients join the ranks of the bullyproof.

SUMMARY

Although this section has concentrated on the bullying side of things it has actually covered a lot of areas that apply in general. People don't often think about the impact of their size, height and shape and how they can intimidate others merely with their physical presence.

You've covered how to play with personal territory and space, using your height, size and shape to your best advantage without overstepping the mark. You've also learned how to deal with anyone who attempts to use these things against you.

Sales and negotiation is a game of brinkmanship. Buyers and sellers alike both have to play the game, which sometimes means using bullying tactics, even if there is no actual physical bullying and, in my experience, many sales people and negotiators actually enjoy this part of their business.

9

THE BODY LANGUAGE OF MANAGING OTHERS

THE MANAGER'S ROLE

Managing others can take a variety of guises: the local cub pack has a leader who manages other volunteers, parents' help and the children attending. The local football club might have a team captain whose job is to manage the players. In business the term 'manager' covers many roles and is often prefaced with a definition of that role: team manager, sales manager, accounts manager, HR manager or general manager.

General manager is about as high a manager as you can get in most companies without being a director. The buck normally stops with the general manager, who usually reports directly to the board.

A manager is simply someone who has been given responsibility for the smooth running of a team, department or company. They generally have a higher level of power within the organization to make decisions.

If you are a manager it is usually your job to look after your staff and report to your superiors on the progress of your team, department or company.

There is an art to being a good manager regardless of your industry. If you have people to manage then you have to be all things to all of them.

- A listening ear when they have problems.

- A disciplinarian when they are constantly late.

- A motivator when they are slipping behind.

- A breaker of bad news and enforcer of policy.

- A mother, brother, father, sister, aunt, uncle and friend all rolled into one.

Managing people is about getting them to do what you and the company need them to do, on time. If you can't, then you are not a manager of people.

Playing all those different roles isn't easy. All too often, people are promoted to the position of manager because they're good at doing a particular job function, rather than some innate ability for the role.

It's very simple. Most people aren't trained to be a manager of staff. They are trained in the job they are good at.

Being a good manager requires many different talents. The skills, knowledge and experience you bring from your actual job function aren't enough.

BODY LANGUAGE ON TV

If you really want to see people managing situations both correctly and incorrectly, watch programmes like *The Apprentice*. You will see a vast array of body language signals from each candidate, some of which work, some of which don't.

In the UK version you have Sir Alan Sugar and in the US, Donald Trump. If you watch both of them you will notice they are very aware of each candidate's body language in the boardroom situation. They will often pick up on a negative movement or gesture and probe the candidate further, which usually results in them digging themselves into a hole.

The negative that they pick up on is not always coming from what the candidate says. More often than not it is a momentary look or roll of the eyes from one of their rivals for the job.

Understanding body language is essential if you are a manager. Your body language tells your team whether you are serious or not when you ask them to do something for you.

If they pick up signs of weakness then you'll lose their respect and you won't get the results you need.

Continue down this path and, eventually, your ability will be called into question by your superiors. It's your job that will be under threat, not your reports, if the work you need to get done isn't happening.

Empathy

Your role as a manager is to manage staff and the day-to-day situations that arise, keeping them on track to meet deadlines, productivity or sales quotas.

As if that isn't enough to contend with, there are always issues going on outside work in people's personal lives that play a vital role and can dictate how your staff behave while doing their job.

Your role includes listening to your staff's concerns about issues arising at work as well as personal things outside.

Whilst most outside problems are not for you to solve, giving your staff the feeling that you are supportive is important. Why?

Because every member of staff you lose means you then have to spend time finding new staff to replace them. That can cost a fortune in advertising, recruitment, training and, more importantly, your time.

The best way to avoid all this is by building rapport, and one of the best ways to do that is by showing empathy and concern. Rapport will help you get people to open up to you, regardless of whether the problems are work related or not.

You can't *make* people talk. Some just don't like to speak up to management, preferring to keep issues to themselves, but when it affects work, you have to at least try.

Playing the role of listener

An empathetic listener will be far more successful in getting people to talk than someone who lacks that skill. There are several body language techniques that can be used to increase empathy.

- *Eye contact*: make more eye contact when you are the listener than the talker.

- *Facial expressions*: use as appropriate to the situation being discussed.

- *Yes/no signals*: nod or shake your head in all the right places to show you are listening.

- *Head tilt*: tilt your head slightly to one side as you listen.

- *Touch*: if appropriate show caring with a touch to back of hand, forearm, upper arm or shoulder.

Discipline

Unfortunately, life as a manager isn't always about showing your caring side. Sometimes it's a case of laying down the law. If staff don't follow the rules then you as their line manager will also have to handle disciplinary procedures, issue warnings and even handle dismissals.

Playing the role of disciplinarian

You can use body language to reinforce your message, so that what your body says is consistent with your words. This way, you will get your message across more clearly, and be taken more seriously.

- *Seating*: in this instance, barriers are good. Set up the room so that you have barriers. A desk is always good, and make sure their chair is smaller than yours with no arm rests. If you have arm rests sit with your elbows out.

- *Eye contact*: instead of your normal eye contact keep it to a minimum. (If you really need to apply some pressure, look at a spot just above the bridge of their nose or on their forehead. This has an amazing effect at making people pay attention. This technique is used a lot in hypnosis.)

- *Facial expression*: serious, no smiles, keep your lips together when you're not speaking.

- *Head angle*: keep it straight both horizontally and vertically. Be careful not to shake or nod your head in the wrong places, which would show agreement.

- *Touch*: apart from maybe a handshake, no touching.

You can also use height – you can seat them whilst you remain standing – and don't forget there is also the *anchoring* you read about earlier. As a manager you should have ample opportunity to set up anchors in your staff both positive and negative.

Remember, you don't always play the nice role, so setting up negative anchors is useful too. For example, the forehead gaze, crossed arms with fingers under armpits and thumbs up, and a slightly raised chin. Put them all together and you have a pattern that your staff will immediately recognize.

CUSTOMER SERVICE

Most of the time when customer service issues are dealt with on a face-to-face basis it is in a shop, restaurant or trade business. The two most common areas of complaint are staff performance and quality of food or goods.

Remember the Pomodoro story? That showed body language in customer service at its best. Good customer service encompasses many different areas but essentially it boils down to one thing: customer satisfaction.

The satisfaction bit is when you get it all right; and the flipside – customer dissatisfaction – comes from getting it wrong. We're going to look at them both but from different perspectives.

Before we look at dealing with problems, let's see how you can give good service from the start.

Customer satisfaction

Giving good customer service starts with body language. After all, that's what customers generally see even before you interact with them verbally.

Let's assume you're running a shop. If the first thing your potential customers see when they come in are two teenage staff sat behind a counter with their mobile phones out, it doesn't exactly encourage the customer to feel like they can interact.

The message it sends is:

'I've got far too much time on my hands and I'm not interested in you'.

I'm sure you will have experienced something like this. It is exactly this sort of negative behaviour that people talk about to their friends, which spreads by word of mouth.

There is a widely held belief in the customer service industry that every bad customer experience gets told to five people, who then tell another five each.

That's around thirty potential or existing customers who could be influenced by one single bad experience.

However, this scenario can be changed into a more positive experience with just the most basic body language acknowledgement. A simple bit of eye contact, a genuine smile, a slight upward tilt of the head and a quick eyebrow flash says:

'Hi, I'm here and quite friendly so just ask if you need any assistance'.

Which would you prefer?

Good customer service is not rocket science. If a customer is going to spend money with your company then their experience has to be good, if not excellent.

Remember, there is very little in this world that a customer can't go to a competitor for. Everyone has competitors – if you don't you are a rare organization indeed. Don't sit back on your laurels thinking it doesn't matter; it does. Just because you don't have a competitor now doesn't mean there isn't one just starting round the corner.

A fact of business is that people go from one company to another. It is how most people progress in their careers; they take over a leaver's role or they go elsewhere to take on new responsibilities. Very few people stay with the same company from school to retirement any more.

People also leave to start their own company. If they do, they know all the mistakes their present employer makes. They only have to correct a few minor hiccups and it becomes possible for them to take over the customer base. Unless your company only sells products and services via the telephone, mail order or internet then chances are there has to be some face-to-face human interaction involved, which always starts with a greeting. A good one can make or break whatever is about to follow.

Make your customers feel important. They are. Without them you have no money to pay salaries and you go bust. If you have staff whose job it is to interact with your customers, make sure they are at least trained in basic body language skills and understand what you expect from them. As the old saying goes: *actions speak louder than words*.

In customer service terms it is always actions that people want. It's what they are paying you for – every business is paid on the basis of doing something and yours is no different.

Customer dissatisfaction

Even when things do go wrong, which let's face it they do, it is always action the customer requires. The way you deal with their dissatisfaction can mean the difference between keeping that customer or losing them to one of your competitors.

Dealing with dissatisfied customers starts again with the greeting, so making sure yours and your staff's greeting is good is important, very important. Here are some simple strategies you can follow.

Disarm and calm

If the customer is in view of other customers then the first thing to do is to try to guide them away to a place where they are less visible.

If they are standing up, get them to sit down, if possible. Sitting has a calming effect on most people. Otherwise they may 'stand their ground' or 'dig their heels in', in which case they probably won't give you the opportunity to put things right for them.

Calming an angry or frustrated customer starts with staying calm yourself. If you match anger with anger you won't get very far.

Most people's anger is not personal, it only becomes personal if you allow it to. By calming someone as quickly as you can, you avoid the situation turning into a scene.

Show empathy expressions as they talk and acknowledge their complaint. Acknowledging is not admitting you are in the wrong;

it just shows you understand where they are coming from and are not dismissing it out of hand.

If all else fails, use double-handed palms together in a praying or pleading gesture to appeal to their emotional side.

SUMMARY

Everyone is managing their daily routines to get to work on time, get the work done and keep the bosses happy. The bosses are managing the staff with managers that have different titles attached and the staff are managing those managers by keeping them happy. Everyone is a manager.

A good manager is someone who always appears to do the right thing at the right time. Managing perceptions is probably a better way to put it, as you don't always have to get things right, but you have to appear to do so.

Whatever you are managing, your job function is to keep your team on track and your bosses happy. The vast majority of this role involves managing perceptions and that can be taken care of in most cases by your own confidence.

When it comes to customer service the basic rule is: get it right first time, by making sure you engage with your customers with your body language even if you can't always get to speak with them first.

When you do speak, continue to use the right body language to appear attentive and make them feel at ease in your company.

10

PUTTING IT ALL TOGETHER

You're very nearly at the end of your learning and it's now time to start linking it all up and using it to your best advantage. In this final chapter I am going to pose a question, and the answers you give will make everything you've learned fit.

Then I'll introduce you to the PIN Code, which is a simple but effective learning aid; then you are on your own to practise what you have learned.

THE ASK QUESTION

I now have one simple question to ask. The answers you give will prove beyond any shadow of a doubt how important body language is in everyday life, especially in business. Before I ask the question, let me set the scene a little first.

Let's just imagine that you have just been selected by your boss to set up a new department in the company you work for. Or, if you prefer, imagine you've got a great idea, seen a gap in the market and want to set up your own business.

Now let's imagine you need to employ 30 staff to help you run this imaginary department or company.

The exercise you need to do is to ask yourself, what are the qualities, traits, skills, knowledge that you want in these new staff you are going to employ? Remember that you will have to work with these people for the next six months, year, two years, three years, maybe even five years plus.

Think carefully before committing to your answers and come up with a list of at least twenty things you believe you want in your new staff. For example, you may list punctual, smart, accurate, team player and so on.

THE ANSWERS

When you've written the list down, or mulled it over in your head, check off each answer on your list against the following and mark it in one of the following categories:

- A = ATTITUDE

- S = SKILL

- K = KNOWLEDGE

Now add up the number of A, S and K answers to find out in your own opinion what is most important to you.

Whenever I give presentations and ask this question, the same sort of answers pop up again and again regardless of industry, job, sex, age, race or anything else. Here's a typical list:

- accurate

- ambitious

- articulate

- committed

- communicative

- confident

- dedicated

- diligent

- energetic

- enthusiastic

- experienced

- fit and healthy

- flexible

- good sense of humour

- hardworking

- honest

- humorous

- innovative

- interpersonal skills

- literate

- loyal

- open minded

- positive

- reliable

- team player.

You'll find that most of these answers are attitude based which, quite simply, means the overriding answer to the question is that attitude counts more than anything else. It comes out top every single time I've done this exercise.

Skill and knowledge never come close to attitude, even though most people believe that those are the things employers want most.

Well, of course they do, but with the right attitude you can find or develop the skills and knowledge to do anything.

ATTITUDE

So why do I mention attitude now and place such importance on it?

Attitude is what you've been learning to observe and read through a person's body language: their attitude towards you and what you have to say, their attitude towards co-workers, managers, customers, the department, the company and everything else in between.

Attitude is what you see in people's reactions to those around them. All the silent clues are there to show how a person feels about what it is they are seeing, hearing, smelling, tasting or touching.

The body language tells you how people feel moment by moment, their attitudes and emotions towards you, the environment and what you have to say.

In business, reading these signs is a crucial skill. Read the signals incorrectly or, worse still, fail to notice them at all, and you lose in the long run.

Knowledge and skills are of course important but not much use unless you can communicate them to others. It is sharing of knowledge and skill with the right attitude that makes things happen.

THE PIN CODE

I mentioned earlier about a code I used to use when I first started with body language and I've certainly used it when I've been analyzing guests on the *Trisha* show or other live TV programmes where instant feedback comments are required.

It's pretty simple really. I've called it the PIN Code because I use it to break down movements into positive, indifferent and negative.

Here's a list of twenty to get you started. Obviously I suggest you make up your own for whatever you want to call each action; as long as *you* know what it means that's all that really counts.

Action	Code	Positive	Indifferent	Negative
Ankle cross	AX			
Arm cross *	AC			
Body posture	BP			
Covering throat	CT			
Cutting/chopping hands	CH			
Eye contact	EC			
Fingers interlink	FI			
Hand shake **	HS			
Head down	HD			
Head tilt	HT			
Incongruent 'No'	IN			
Incongruent 'Yes'	IS			
Leaning back	LB			
Leaning in	LI			
Open palms	OP			
Palms hidden	PH			
Pointed finger	PF			
Raised heels	RH			
Self comforting	SC			
Smiles	SM			
Steepled fingers	SF			
Wagging finger ***	WF			

* You can add an extra CF=Clenched fists, RH=Relaxed hands, GA= Gripping arms TU=Thumbs up
** You can add an extra PD=Palm down, PU=Palm up or PV=Palm vertical
*** You can add SS=Side-to-side, UD= Up and down

PRACTICE, PRACTICE, PRACTICE

In most big money sports matches the difference between coming in first or second is huge, both in terms of pride and prowess, but also in financial terms.

The winner can often pocket more than ten times as much as the runner up. Does that mean the winner is ten times better than the runner up? No. In most cases it just means the winner had a tiny advantage. That's all it takes in business to really excel over your competition, whether they are

- fellow workers seeking promotion,

- another company selling the same product, service, concept, or

- your industry's achievement awards.

So use what you've learned here and practise. Look all around you. TV is a wonderful window on the world with hundreds of channels available at the touch of a button. Record a programme and watch it with the sound off while it's recording. Make notes on what you pick up from the actors' body language about their attitudes, emotions and what you think they're expressing. Then watch it again with the sound up and see how closely what you observed and noted matches with what is actually going on.

This way you also learn to pick up on new things you maybe didn't first time round. You can then watch for them in future.

- *Soap operas.* These are great because the actors tend to overact their parts slightly so you get emphasis on facial expressions, body postures, hand gestures and all the other things you've covered so far.

- *Political.* Live political debates are also an excellent observation point, particularly when politicians are having to answer questions thrown at them by the general public. Watch for defensiveness, openness, deception, incomplete gestures and signals.

- *Reality shows.* These are great for observing reactions to unusual situations. Most of these types of show throw curve balls at the weird and wonderful participants – giving them strange tasks, things to wear, different roles to play and all sorts.

Watch live events back in slow motion and you'll find you pick up even more, particularly micro facial expressions and quick body movements like shoulder shrugs and elbow flicks, which are often missed under normal circumstances.

Away from the TV there are three more areas for observing people easily.

- *Work.* Your own workplace is brilliant because here you get to observe people over long periods of time and can really pick up when their moods are good, bad, happy, sad. You can then choose the right time to approach them when you want them to do things for you.

- *Family and friends.* As with the workplace you can observe people over longer periods. You may never have actually taken any notice of how your family and friends react to things. All I can say is, start, because you can always question these people to confirm or deny your observations.

- *Public areas.* Virtually any bar, restaurant, coffee shop, nightclub or shopping centre is a good place to sit back and watch people. If you go to different sorts of places you should notice different behaviours that are influenced by the environment itself. Go to the public gallery in a court of law, a sports club viewing gallery, etc. See what patterns you observe in one place that you do or don't see in another.

You may have just read this book for fun and never intend on using the knowledge it contains. That's entirely your choice. However, I would encourage you to go and play with what you've learned. It is the only way to find out what works best for you in different situations.

If you don't then you will never know how much more success-ful you could be with the people you meet and deal with daily in your chosen industry. Just by changing a few small things here and there and learning from the results you can increase your own self-confidence

CONFIDENCE AND POWER: WHAT IS CONFIDENCE?

This is an amazingly complex question to answer and people have completely differing views of what confidence actually is. I ask the question often at my seminars and I'm always surprised at the answers.

Whatever confidence is, it feeds into every area of your life. You can be confident in one area but not another. Some people are very confident in their jobs but ask them to do something outside their normal role and they lose it.

At some level, confidence is your belief in your own abilities, knowledge and skills about what you are capable of doing.

Some people seem confident in all areas but I can assure you they are not. These people will have their own set of insecurities in areas you don't know about.

There is an interesting piece of research by Joseph Luft and Harry Ingham, known as 'Johari's window'.

Essentially it breaks down into four sections – or windows – of known and unknown information about you:

1.   information known by you and others

2.   information known to others but not you

3.   information not known by you or others

4.   information you know that others don't.

In brief, you don't know what others know about you, nor do they know what you know about them. Consequently, where you believe you are confident, others may think differently because they see things in you that you don't. How could you? Unless you have a film crew following you round all day, every day, videoing every situation you find yourself in, you will never get the full picture.

For me, confidence is simply feeling comfortable with yourself in any situation you find yourself in, and being able to admit when you're wrong with grace and sincerity.

That covers it all I think.

It's not having to know everything.

It's not being the life and soul.

It's just feeling comfortable with yourself, with whoever, wherever.

Confidence in certain areas has a truly beguiling effect on people. They will do just about anything for someone exhibiting ultimate confidence in what they say and do.

You will be amazed when you start to experiment with what you've learned in this book, at just how much people will do for you if you present yourself in a confident enough manner.

There have been, and still are, many experiments and studies conducted on the incredible influence confidence has over others. Two examples spring to mind.

The first took place in the US, where a man crossed the road when the 'Don't Walk' sign was on, which is known as 'jaywalking'. It's an offence in many states in the US, as it is in lots of other countries around the world.

The first time he did it he was dressed up in a suit, shirt and tie carrying a briefcase and looking confident. The bystanders waiting to cross followed him.

The second time he did the same thing but was dressed in scruffy old jeans, T-shirt and trainers. Guess what? No one followed him.

Another famous experiment was conducted by Stanley Milgram of Yale University, and is known as the Milgram experiment. Pairs of volunteers were selected to take two different roles: teacher and learner. These were supposedly chosen at random by drawing lots. However, the volunteer was always selected as the teacher – the role of learner was actually played by an actor.

The teacher and learner were put in separate rooms where they could hear but not see each other. The teacher had to read out a series of word pairs for the learner to memorize. The teacher then tested the learner by reading out the first word in each pair and offering four possible answers. If the learner gave the correct answer, nothing happened, but if they were wrong, the teacher would administer an electric shock, which increased in power with each wrong answer. At least, that's what the teacher was told. In fact, the learner wasn't receiving any shocks at all but was instructed to act as if they were.

There is another critical component to the experiment: in the room with the teacher was an official, helping to conduct the experiment. This official was crucial because, as each scream of pain got louder and more intense, some of the teachers would resist giving the next shock. As far as they were concerned they were administering bigger and bigger electric shocks each time. The official, however, would encourage them to continue, telling them it was fine, even when the shocks supposedly being administered were potentially fatal. Many of the teachers continued to push the button and give the shocks.

This experiment, which has been replicated many times all around the world, tests the theory that people will go as far as administering deadly electric shocks to another human being if told to do so by an official.

Not everyone did go all the way and virtually everyone playing the teacher role, whether they went to the maximum or not, showed signs of stress in doing the experiment.

However, a massive 61–66% people would go to the max and all because of a person with a clipboard, white coat, a bit of confidence and all its associated power.

CONFIDENCE = POWER AND TRUST

These two examples should give you a sense of how important confidence is when dealing with others, particularly in business.

It works in two ways. When people have confidence in you, they trust you and expect you to deliver on time, every time.

If you do, they gain more trust and confidence in you. This is basically how promotion works in most companies and how most companies grow in their industry.

It also works in another way too. It gives you power because, as the Milgram experiment shows, you can use confidence and trust to get others to do things for you, or to allow you to do things without question. There are frequent news stories of crooks pulling off crimes by sheer brass-neck confidence.

Hypnosis works a lot of the time purely because of the trust and confidence the client has in the hypnotherapist.

Confidence in business can take you a long way even without the necessary abilities, knowledge or skill.

How you get it

You gain confidence from the feedback you get from others and the feedback you give yourself.

Remember I talked about growing up in a safe or unsafe environment as a child? Well, that's where a lot of it starts. The feedback you got from your parents, siblings, grandparents, teachers. You do well at something and you get good feedback. You do not so well and you get negative feedback.

This feedback from others can often dictate how confident you are in different areas of your life.

Negative feedback is not always a bad thing, however. It can be just as beneficial as positive feedback if you are able to use a negative experience as a way to learn and develop. Many of us, though, won't attempt anything that might cause pain – we like to stay within our comfort zones.

> 'If you keep on doing what you've always done, you'll keep on getting what you've always got.'
>
> *W. L. Bateman*

Your body language is a major part of how confident you appear to others. If you carry on doing what you've always done with your body then you will continue to get the same results you always have and nothing changes.

Change for most people is scary, but by changing small things and observing how people react, you can build up your confidence bit by bit.

If you are lucky enough to be confident already then good for you. You will have no problem making small changes and noticing the difference, whether positive or negative.

As for confidence, it is for the most part nothing more than trying something new and learning from it. The more you learn about reading other people, the more confident you will become in yourself with whoever, wherever, whenever.

BODY LANGUAGE – WRAPPING IT ALL UP

In any job, there are people you have to interact with on a daily basis. You simply must engage with others in order to get things done and move forward.

If you can understand what people are telling you with their body and not just their mouths, you place yourself in a very strong position. Let's face it, no matter how much you'd like to be friendly and get on with each another, ultimately your responsibility is to do the best you can for your employer.

That is how the company moves forward. You keep your job and the company continues to pay your salary each month.

If you're in any sort of sales role you don't immediately give the lowest price you can for your brand new 'megatech widget and service pack'. No, you try to get the most out of it by negotiating, so that it's a good deal for the customer and a good deal for your company – hence the expression 'win–win'. Otherwise your company will go to the wall, and you will have no job and no salary.

If you're the manager of a department full of staff, it is your responsibility to get the best out of your team: to get them to buy into their role fully within the department and into the department's role within the company.

Whenever you give a presentation the idea is to share knowledge and get the audience to buy into your product or service.

When politicians speak the idea is to get voters to buy into the values and policies of their party.

Business makes the world go round and keeps the money in your pocket. Whether you like it or not, for the most part, it's like a game of poker and you are a player. Being able to read when someone is bluffing, lying, holding back, or being deceptive is essential to your success. Most of the time critical body movements, signals and gestures are all there for you to observe and decode.

Unfortunately, face-to-face meetings are getting fewer and fewer the more we rely on technology. Mobile phones, voicemails, emails, video conferencing – all of these basically prevent real human interaction between two or more people.

When you meet people face-to-face you see their reactions. Even if you've never studied anything to do with body language before, you get a sense about them and the meeting.

You get feedback when you're actually with people that you simply don't get on the phone or by leaving a message on voicemail. You get the words and the tonality but you do not get the full picture.

Email has developed its own visual language for expressing emotion – emoticons – but they are a poor substitute.

Video conferencing is about the best of the lot, but it still falls way short of actually meeting people face-to-face. It's nigh impossible to capture every single member of a group on a video screen and frequently the camera is set way too far back for you to see expressions or small movements. They tell you so much more about a person or a group's attitude towards the topic being discussed.

Attitudes are feelings both expressed and unexpressed.

Everything you do in life is to create feeling. All our decisions are based on feelings or what Sigmund Freud called the 'Pleasure Pain Principle'.

Feelings are extremely important when it comes to reading people and their body language. Feelings are exactly what they are expressing to you non-verbally, whether they want to or not.

Some people are more expressive with their body than others, just like some people talk more than others.

It doesn't matter though – everyone expresses their emotions, feelings and attitudes through their body language.

SUMMARY

Congratulations and well done! You made it to the end, so, what now?

My advice is don't stop here. Actually play with what you've learned with family, friends and close business colleagues, and then get their feedback. Learn what works for you and put it to use to take your relationships and career to another level.

Although we've gone through a lot of information on the subject there is more; much more. I've only covered a small fraction of the possible meanings behind the movements, signals and gestures. It would be impossible to cover the whole subject in just one book when you consider that, according to Mario Pei, you have more than 700,000 possible signals. Add to that a possible 250,000 facial expressions as estimated by Ray Birdwhistle, more than 5000 distinct hand movements indicated in research by M.H. Krout, and studies by G.W. Hughes, which show over 1000 ways to sit and stand.

If you are any sort of mathematician then you can work out the possible combinations of those figures and you'll come up with something that doesn't fit on most calculators, a figure in the trillions. I came up with 875,000,000,000,000,000!

You are now on your way to becoming more observant with the people you meet every single day. You should now understand that all your emotions essentially control how you present yourself to the world and why you get the reactions you get from people.

Good luck.

Robert

THE BACK STORY
– *YOU'RE LYING*
– HOW IT ALL
STARTED

How did I become interested in body language?

It's a fair question and one I'm asked on a regular basis because, let's face it, earning your living doing what I do is a little unusual.

Well the truth is that I was caught lying! My own body language gave me away, which had quite a profound effect on the young 20-year-old me. More than 25 years ago, I went to an interview for a job as a sales representative selling Canon photocopiers. It was all arranged a bit last minute so I was wearing a shirt, jacket and tie looking smart but it wasn't a suit.

I walked through the door for the interview, shook the guy's hand and was immediately asked if I had a suit.

'Yes' I said confidently.

'Why aren't you wearing it then?

'It's at the cleaners.'

'You're lying but I like your answer. Sit down.'

I just been caught out lying in an instant. My one and only suit was a crumpled mess at the bottom of my bed. You see, I was out of work at the time and had no plans for this interview that was forced on me by my mother trawling the local papers to get me a job and out from under her feet.

I must have done OK throughout the 45 minute interview because they offered me the job at the end of it, which I gratefully accepted. But I kept thinking, 'How did he (Iain Grant) know I was lying just like that?'

So I asked him.

'Your body language gave you away.'

'My what?'

You see, no one had ever put those two words – body and language – together before that moment, so it meant nothing to me.

Now that may sound ridiculous in this day and age, but you have to remember this was more than 25 years ago and those two words had only just been married together.

This was so fascinating to me I went on a quest to find out more but, unfortunately for me at that time, there was very little out there for me to get my hands on. These are four books that I could get hold of in 1984:

- Desmond Morris, *The Naked Ape* (1967)

- Desmond Morris, *Manwatching* (1979)

- Julius Fast, *Body Language* (1979)

- Allan Pease, *Body Language* (1981)

The secrets these first few books revealed made me even more fascinated by the subject and, now that I was in sales, I had the perfect playground to test out all the things I'd been reading about. And I did. Deliberately, consciously changing my body language in certain situations or at certain points in meetings.

Later on, as my career progressed, I started training and managing new salespeople coming through the ranks. Now, one thing about salesmen and saleswomen is that they come from all sorts of backgrounds and very few of them began with the intention of becoming a salesperson. I myself didn't plan on going into sales prior to getting that first selling job with Mr Grant. I'd been a bailiff and a private detective.

Yes, you read that right: I was a private detective.

At the tender age of 19 years old I was running a private detective agency from within a company of certificated bailiffs. I worked for WJ Gault & Co (now named Gaults the bailiffs).

After spending a year in the office learning the administrative role behind the scenes I began to go out with senior bailiffs to learn how they actually went about the job of collecting debts on behalf of local councils, landlords and businesses. A bailiff's job is a series of face-to-face interactions involving bluff, deceit, negotiation and closing.

All of this set me up well to secure my sales rep post with Mr Grant, despite being caught out lying at the very start of my interview.

I spent 15 years selling, managing and training people for the likes of Canon, Agfa, Xerox, Hewlett-Packard and Apple, to name but a few. During this time, I continued to read, watch and learn as much as I could about reading people. I literally knocked on thousands of office doors in London, Kent, Surrey, Sussex and Essex, talking to receptionists one minute and managing directors the next. I had to be able to read and act differently depending on who I was talking to and why.

Reading people became an essential skill. To get it wrong was to get nowhere, but if I read them right I usually ended up with deal and a decent commission.

So, you can see why it became important for me to become skilled at reading people. My life literally depended on it now – it was keeping a roof over my head and the food in my belly.

Having spent all this time learning, playing, selling, training and honing my body language skills, I decided in October 1999 that it was time to set up my own training company and go teach others what I'd learned.

It kicked off in January 2000 and, by May, I had a business partner called John. We struggled for that first year because, although John was now a partner, he was still working full time for someone else so he had very little time or involvement.

We needed help to get established or it was going to fall flat on its face, my dreams would be over and I'd be back working for someone else just like John. I didn't ever want to have to go back and work for someone else.

Who on earth could we turn to for help with this fledgling company? Allan Pease, I thought.

I pestered his office until eventually I got an appointment to go see him and his lovely wife Barbara at their English home in the beautiful Warwickshire countryside. This, to me, was no ordinary meeting. I was about to come face-to-face with a person who, 17 years earlier, had ignited an interest that was to take me on a fascinating journey of discovery.

The meeting must have gone OK because we left with a deal to promote Allan's work. I knew this would open doors but not in a way that I even dreamed about: television.

I was sitting in my office one Tuesday afternoon in April 2002 when the phone rang:

'Hi, this is Emma Martins from ITV's *Trisha* show and I'm trying to get hold of Allan Pease.'

'OK, tell me more and I'll do all I can to assist', I said – or words to that effect.

It turned out they wanted Allan to read the body language of guests on one of the shows on the Friday of that week. I explained that it was highly unlikely that he'd be able to make it as his schedule was booked months in advance but that I would get in contact with his office and let them know. Then, without really thinking I said:

'If Allan can't do it you can always come back to me and I'll see if I can help you out.'

I duly contacted Allan's office and passed on the contact details of the TV company with a rough explanation of what they wanted and when. They spoke with each other and the next thing I knew I was speaking on the phone with the same woman, who was saying:

'We've spoken with Allan's office and he can't make it so they've recommended we contact you to do it, can you come to our studio in Norwich and read the body language of the guests on our show?'

'Errr, yes.'

That was it. I'd just said yes to doing a TV show with a live audience – a show that I'd never watched before (except a few snippets I'd caught when channel hopping). I didn't even know what the show was about.

I arrived at the studio and was ushered into a room where I was kept until it was time for me to do my thing, except for a little 30-second video trailer they asked me to do, in which I introduced myself and what I'd be doing in the show. I deliberately chose the wording:

'Hello, I'm Robert Phipps, body language expert for the Trisha show.'

There is nothing TV loves more than an expert to cast an opinion on something – anything. Be it football, politics, business or relationships, TV has an expert for everything.

Sitting in the little room they'd put me in to hide me out of the way until the show started, I knew with every fibre of my body that if I messed this up there was no going back. I had sweaty palms, armpits and top lip. I was hot and my heart was pounding away but I couldn't let them see that I was nervous. I had to use all my skills just to keep control of my own body language and to exude confidence.

Yes, I'd done TV before but *Trisha* was different, very different. This had a live audience, this had guests that I had to comment on, and if I thought they were lying I had to say so, which is a very strange position to find yourself in. Sitting in judgement over someone and basing your evaluation solely on their body language and whether or not it, in your opinion, matches the words that are coming out of their mouths.

As much as I was terrified before the show started, I still managed to thoroughly enjoy myself during the recording and almost managed to forget about the nerves. Once I was busy watching the guests, I entered a different world: I was in analytical mode, which took all my concentration. I didn't want to miss a single muscle twitch, fake smile or shrug of the shoulders.

As it turned out, my appearance on the show was a success and I ended up as the resident body language expert on the *Trisha Goddard Show* for seven years and lost count of how many shows I actually ended up doing after the first hundred!

I became known as 'The Human Lie Detector' because, after I'd make my judgement call of liar or truth teller, that guest would be taken off to do a full blown polygraph lie detector test with Bruce Burgess, one of this country's leading polygraphers. Lucky for me I rarely got it wrong.

That massive exposure not only put my work up for scrutiny by everyone, it also opened other doors for TV work. The Big Brother studios came calling, so did *This Morning*. These three TV shows were huge and watched by millions, which opened even more doors from newspapers and magazines to the news on the BBC, Sky, GMTV – analysing celebrities, politicians and anyone else who found themselves in the media spotlight.

Over the last ten years, the body language I have written about has gone beyond just a passion and led me down paths I could never have imagined. It's given me the opportunity to work with some great people and to impart some of my knowledge, which in turn has helped them in all sorts of areas of their lives. Hopefully it'll do the same for you. Have fun.

THANKS

The writing of this book is down to the people I've met over the years. It simply would not have been possible without them. With that in mind I would like to thank, personally, the thousands of clients, colleagues, family and friends who've helped me learn most without even realizing it – whilst I experimented with all the different things that I've covered in these pages.

I'd like to extend much appreciation to Barbara & Allan Pease for allowing me to sell and promote their products right at the beginning and for referring the Trisha team on to me when they couldn't make that very first program in which I took their place.

A big 'Thank you' to Trisha and all the crews I had the pleasure to work with. They looked after me wonderfully and made me feel part of the show – right from the start to the very end, seven years later.

My gorgeous daughter, Gemma, for not killing or excommunicating me forever for being a tired old grouch during the writing of this book!

And, finally, my greatest gratitude goes to my wonderful wife, Mariann. For more than 25 years she has put up with me scrutinizing her every move – and every move of her friends too. She has tolerated my endless observations on the behaviour of others whilst out shopping, eating, on the beach – and everywhere else. She's also sat up late into the early hours for many nights helping me do the final edits for this book, which wasn't easy.

Thank you all,
Robert

ABOUT
ROBERT PHIPPS

Robert Phipps is one of the UK's best known body language experts and has given his commentary and analysis of all the major party political leaders. A renowned international platform speaker and trainer, Robert is in constant demand by both the media and business worlds. He has written and commented for almost every national newspaper and magazine in the UK and has contributed to many trade-specific journals both here and abroad. Robert was also the resident body language expert on the *Trisha Goddard Show* for more than seven years with well over 100 appearances on the show, as well as being guest analyst on *Big Brother's Little Brother*.

Robert has worked on a wide range of projects with the Lone Workers Safety Conference, LA Childrens Hospital, Global Tolerance, Association of Pet Behaviour Counsellors, the Society of Occupational Medicine and the Institute of Business Advisors, to name a few. He is also the co-author of several books including *101 Great Ways To Improve Your Life Volume 2* and *Be Safe – The Guide to Women's Personal Safety*.

For more information, go to www.robertphipps.com or contact Robert at:

Facebook: Robert Phipps
Twitter: @robertphipps
Email: robert@robertphipps.com
Tel: +44 (0)1233-335078

IMAGE CREDITS

Laughing laptop man – © Jason Stitt/istockphoto.com

Happy senior man wearing a suit – © Carmen Martínez Banús/ istockphoto.com

Elegant woman portrait – © Andreas Rodriguez/istockphoto.com

Little Santa – © Alija/istockphoto.com

Portrait of happy young businessman – © Neustockimages/ istockphoto.com

Beautiful lovable young woman portrait, smiling at camera, hands clasped – © Quavondo/istockphoto.com

Winner success woman – © Ariwasabi/istockphoto.com

Human anatomy – muscles * female head – © Linda Bucklin/istockphoto. com

Disapproving old man glares at camera over his glasses, frowning – © Don Bayley/istockphoto.com

Mature woman portrait – © Rubén Hidalgo/istockphoto.com

Expressive face × 7 – © VikaValter/istockphoto.com

Four interracial female friends laughing and looking at laptop computer – © Darren Baker/istockphoto.com

Coffee conversations – © Joey Boylan/istockphoto.com

Stand off – © Trista Weibell/istockphoto.com

Business people shaking hands – © Szocs Jozsef/istockphoto.com

Business people shaking hands – © Jacob Wackerhausen/istockphoto.com

Friendly hands shake – © Ruslan Dashinsky/istockphoto.com

Double date – © Nuno/istockphoto.com

CHAPTER 5

Portrait of a confident businessman sitting on chair – © Clerkenwell_Images/istockphoto.com

Thoughtful businessman sitting at conference table – © Clerkenwell_Images/istockphoto.com

Businesswoman with folder, isolated on white – © Lsaloni/istockphoto.com

Talking about life – series – © Andreea Erim/istockphoto.com

Anger 2 – © Thomas Perkins/istockphoto.com

Meadow – © Diego Cervo/istockphoto.com

Two women having a fight – © Luba Nel/istockphoto.com

Human hands – © Ragip Candan/istockphoto.com

Hands – © Luke Tan/istockphoto.com

Alone in the city – © Rasmus Rasmussen/istockphoto.com

Elderly man lost in thought – © Jacob Wackerhausen/istockphoto.com

Support – © Wuka/istockphoto.com

Reclining businessman – © Martti Salmela/istockphoto.com

The thinker – © Sturti/istockphoto.com

Cheerful businesswoman with crossed arms – © Lise Gagne/istockphoto.com

Businessmen II – © Lise Gagne/istockphoto.com

Annoyed businessman – © ranplett/istockphoto.com

CHAPTER 6

Business presentation – © Grady Reese/istockphoto.com

Businessman gesturing – © Jacob Wackerhausen/istockphoto.com

Business meeting – © Kemter/istockphoto.com

Two colleagues sitting in business building and looking at camera – © Kristian Sekulic/istockphoto.com

CHAPTER 7

Brain isolated – © James Arrington/istockphoto.com

CHAPTER 8

Smiling man standing in a doorway – © Hiob/istockphoto.com

Woman healthcare worker – © Rich Legg/istockphoto.com

Confident businessman standing behind chair – © Devon Stephens/istockphoto.com

Happy couple embracing – © Daniel Laflor/istockphoto.com

Elderly affectionate couple portrait – © Kevin Russ/istockphoto.com

INDEX